The Bunjee Venture

Look for these and other Apple® Paperbacks in your local bookstore!

The Hairy Horror Trick
   by Scott Corbett
Rich Mitch
   by Marjorie Weinman Sharmat
Short Season
   by Scott Eller
Ghosts Beneath Our Feet
   by Betty Ren Wright
The Dollhouse Murders
   by Betty Ren Wright

The Bunjee Venture

Stan McMurtry

with illustrations by the author

AN
APPLE®
PAPERBACK

SCHOLASTIC INC.
New York Toronto London Auckland Sydney

ISBN 0-590-40396-6

12 11 10 9 8 7 6 5 4 3 2   7 8 9/8 0 1/9

Printed in the U.S.A.

For Maureen, Karen, and Andy
who probably wished at times
that I would build myself a
machine and disappear.

Chapter One

The great silver orb stood gleaming on the cluttered work bench. It balanced precariously on one stout metal leg. A mass of multicoloured wires and tubes wormed their way like tangled spaghetti from points to sockets around one side and long antennae sprouted from the top like two ears alert to catch the smallest sound.

Mr. Winsborrow placed his screwdriver down on the bench and mopped his brow with an oily handkerchief. He stood back a pace and admired his handywork.

"Beautiful! Beautiful!" he murmured and then glancing heavenwards, "This time! Please let it work this time."

He picked up a crumpled blueprint from an untidy heap of blueprints littering the floor and started to check systematically each valve and screw, every wire and plug. Two hours later he sat back tired but satisfied on a wooden box which he used as a stool and lit up his ancient pipe. It did nothing to calm his excitement. The time for testing was here. The time when he would know whether the months of working and planning and putting up with all the family jokes had been worth while.

"Ah well, better get on with it," he thought, and climbing over the piles of bolts and nuts and discarded machinery which were piled high on the garage floor, he went into the house.

Mrs. Winsborrow and the children were in the lounge watching television. It was early evening and a Western film was in full swing. Mrs. Winsborrow was plump and had a jolly face with big blue eyes. She was also a little absent minded. The scarf that she was knitting was already about ten feet long. But it didn't really matter, she just enjoyed knitting. Probably the scarf would go on and on and on until someone hinted that he'd like a pullover or a pair of socks and then she'd drop the scarf and knit an enormous pullover with sleeves that went on and on and on. Her eyes never left the television screen but her fingers knitted on independently.

Karen and Andrew were bright, cheerful children. She was fourteen and madly keen on horses, records, and a spotty faced boy at school. Her brother was twelve years old and was fascinated by mechanical things, motor bikes and television sets, also food, reading, not washing, and staying in bed in the morning. The interest in mechanical things had been fostered by his father. For years they had been happy together tinkering about with car engines or mending the television. But suddenly Mr. Winsborrow had started inventing things. His every spare moment was spent in the garage or at the kitchen table drawing plans or experimenting with electrical apparatus.

So far his inventions included a contraption for taking the top off a boiled egg, which went wrong on the first attempt and pounded the egg, eggcup and a bit of the dining room table into small pieces. Then came a mechanical stirring spoon which clipped on to the side of a saucepan and automatically stirred the contents. This performed beautifully until one day it fell into the saucepan and the soup was served up to guests at dinner with bits of metal cogs and screws mixed with the vegetables and tasting dreadfully of lubricating oil. Mr. Winsborrow had been convinced that he would make his fortune with his next brain-wave, the automatic dog brusher, and had hoped to demonstrate his invention at Crufts dog show. The family did not have a pet dog so on the day of the test he had borrowed their next door neighbour's miniature poodle. The dog was strapped into the device and the automatic brushes were set in motion. Now if Mr. Winsborrow had not been called to the phone just at that moment and if Mrs. Winsborrow had not picked up her knitting and settled down to watch a play on television, then they would not have had the embarrassment of handing back to their next door neighbour a completely bald poodle.

"I have been plagued with sheer bad luck," said Mr. Winsborrow when his wife and children gently teased him about his inventions. "You wait and see, one day I shall be famous for my inventions. One day when we're rich, then you'll regret teasing me."

And so it had gone on. A lawnmower that mowed the lawn on its own and incidentally the flower beds too. An engine which ran on ginger beer. A bed which tipped over at 8 o'clock in the morning thus saving the necessity of buying an alarm clock, and many many more gadgets.

Then suddenly Mr. Winsborrow had become even more busy in the garage. He locked the door behind him and no one was allowed in or even near the place.

Little things from the house had a tendency to disappear mysteriously. The bread bin lid vanished without trace one day. A metal post which held up the corner of the car port also disappeared and the flex from the lamp in the hall went the same way. It was very baffling and also rather annoying that they were not allowed into the secret, but they learned to put up with it and had become used to the fact that they hardly ever saw Mr. Winsborrow except at breakfast times. Occasionally though he would take Andrew and Karen down to the library with him where he would spend hours leafing avidly through heavy scientific books making copious notes and muttering things like "Ooh" or "Aah" or "My goodness, yes of course" to himself and to all their questions and pleas about his latest project would only answer, "You'll see my dears, you'll see."

And see they did that very day. An extremely excited Mr. Winsborrow burst into the lounge, his head smeared with oil from his oily handkerchief and his pipe upside down in his mouth dropping hot ash on to the carpet.

"I've finished," he cried triumphantly, waving his arms in the air. "The greatest invention the world has ever known! I've invented something so incredible, so staggering, that it will astonish and baffle the world's greatest scientists."

"You'll want a cup of tea then I expect," said Mrs. Winsborrow not looking up from the screen.

"Tea? This is no time for tea!" roared Mr. Winsborrow. "I tell you, you are about to see history in the making!" He grabbed his wife by the hand and pulled her up out of her chair and towards the door. The children had already leapt up enthusiastically and were waiting outside the garage door bubbling over with curiosity.

"Hold on my dears," said Mr. Winsborrow, unlocking the garage door. "Your months of patience are about to be rewarded, your every question answered."

He threw open the door with a flourish and helped his wife over the piles of discarded machinery that littered the floor, then he waved his hand in a grand gesture at his latest creation and said, "There! What do you think?" They stared in open-mouthed astonishment at the great globe standing on the workbench, its mass of coloured wires and all the rest of the silver painted, pinned and bolted paraphenalia which made up the weird object that Mr. Winsborrow had called the greatest invention in the world. It was some minutes before anybody spoke and then:

"Here! Isn't that my bread bin lid?" said Mrs. Winsborrow, stepping forward and examining a piece of metal that was welded to the side of the structure.

"Daddy! That's one of my stirrups!" wailed Karen, prodding a finger at another lump of metal stuck to the top.

"And my bicycle pump!" yelled Andy. "I wondered where that had gone." Protruding from the side of the machine was a bank of three piston-like objects, one of which definitely was a bicycle pump.

"Enough! Enough!" cried Mr. Winsborrow. "How can you worry about such trivialities at a time like this? History is about to be made! The whole scientific world about to be shaken to the core and all you can worry about are bread bin lids and bicycle pumps."

"And stirrups!" said Karen.

"It's a peculiar looking machine," said Andy. "What is it? What's it supposed to do?"

11

Karen scratched her head thoughtfully. "I know," she said, "I bet it's a pop music machine. You press a button and you get non-stop pop music all day."

Mr. Winsborrow glanced heavenwards and muttered softly under his breath.

Mrs. Winsborrow clapped her hands together excitedly. "Darling, it's an automatic tea maker!"

The expression on Mr. Winsborrow's face made it clear that it was most definitely not an automatic tea maker.

"It's just a heap of old junk," said Andy.

"This," said Mr. Winsborrow through clenched teeth, "is my time machine."

"Time machine?" they all echoed. "What? Do you mean to say it's just a clock?" said Mrs. Winsborrow.

"Not that kind of time machine, silly." He reached up to the side of the machine and pulled on a small brass handle which Mrs. Winsborrow instantly recognised as being the handle that had been missing for weeks from the kitchen cupboard door.

A small door opened in the side of the machine and Mr. Winsborrow hopped with surprising agility up onto the workbench. He squeezed through the door and sat down on a wooden seat inside. It was a very tight fit. Pressed against his stomach was a stout wooden board onto which was fitted rows and rows of switches and bulbs and dials and levers.

He looked down at their incredulous faces and smiled. "Let me tell you how all this started," he said.

"I think you'd better," said Mrs. Winsborrow. "But hurry up, we're missing a lovely play on the television."

"About eighteen months ago," said Mr. Winsborrow, ignoring her, "I got a book from the library which was really fascinating. It was by a man called H. G. Wells and it was called *The Time Machine*. It was all about a man who invented a marvellous machine in which he could travel through time, forwards into the future or back into history. It was really intriguing. It meant that a man didn't have to rely on history books, but could actually go back in time and check the facts for himself."

Mr. Winsborrow sucked excitedly on his pipe and two great clouds of smoke filled the domed top of his great invention. "Of course it was only a book, an exciting yarn, a figment of the author's imagination and when I'd finished reading it I put it down and forgot all about it for a while. But then one day Karen asked me to help her with her history homework and there was a question I couldn't answer. It suddenly occurred to me how marvellous it would be if a machine such as H. G. Wells had described really existed. Once the thought was in my mind I couldn't get rid of it and so I started working out a method of making solid substances disintegrate and travel through time. It would take too long to explain exactly how it works, but put simply it means travelling along through a beam of light."

"I've never heard anything so ridiculous," said Mrs. Winsborrow. "Travel through time indeed. It's not possible."

"But it is possible," exploded Mr. Winsborrow. "And I shall prove it."

Mrs. Winsborrow folded her ample arms across her chest, leaned against the garage wall and stared at her husband. She didn't say anything, she didn't have to. Her whole attitude said what they were all thinking – "Go on then, prove it."

Mr. Winsborrow frowned determinedly, settled himself with a wriggle firmly into his seat and started switching switches and pressing buttons on the panel before him. Little green and red bulbs lit up above his head and a loud humming noise started from somewhere below the seat. He reached forward and picked up two small plugs which were attached to wires which trailed underneath the panel. He pushed the plugs into his ears. Then reaching behind him he pulled a kind of metal studded seat belt around his chest and clicked it into a socket in the wall.

"All right, where would you like me to go?" he said, glaring down at the unbelievers below.

"Go forward in time a few days," said Mrs. Winsborrow. "And bring back next week's wage packet. I'm a bit short."

"I'm learning about dinosaurs at school," said Andy. "Go back to the days when dinosaurs were alive and then come back and tell us all about it."

"Right," said Mr. Winsborrow. "Let's see now, that would be about one hundred and twenty million years ago."

He turned a small pointer around on a dial in front of him. The dial was marked off in units of a million. One to a hundred. Next to that was another dial marked off in thousands, then another in hundreds, then two more in tens and single units. Beside all these dials was a small lever. Above the lever was printed the word "PAST" and below the lever was the word "FUTURE". He pressed the lever up. Instantly the machine started to vibrate violently. The humming noise changed to a high pitched whine and blue and yellow electrical flashes sparked furiously between the two antennae on the roof.

Mrs. Winsborrow stepped forward anxiously. "Be careful dear," she cried. "It doesn't look safe standing on just that one leg." Indeed the machine was shaking so violently that it looked as though it might fall off the workbench.

"Don't worry!" shouted Mr. Winsborrow above the noise. "Here I go." He stabbed his finger down on a large red button in the panel and closed the door with a slam. Too big a slam. The machine, already lurching and vibrating, seemed to feel the bang of the door just as a tired boxer feels a hard blow to the body. Slowly it keeled over sideways, thudded over onto the workbench, scattering tools everywhere, then crashed down onto the garage floor where it lay shuddering like a stricken animal. Two great puffs of smoke belched out from its sides, the whine of the engines stopped abruptly and then it lay still.

Mrs. Winsborrow and the children rushed forward horrified. Karen grasped the door handle and tried to pull it open. There was a blinding flash and with an almighty bang the machine exploded. All three of them were hurled through the air in a welter of bolts, nuts and bits of wire, to thud painfully against the wall of the garage. They scrambled up again in panic and fear, tearing at the wreckage littered around them.

"Arthur! Arthur! Are you all right?" screamed Mrs. Winsborrow.

"Daddy!" shouted the children.

They rushed across to the workbench where the smoking and broken husk of the machine lay, and then around the garage frantically searching and calling. But although they searched the small garage for two more hours, of Mr. Winsborrow there was not the slightest trace.

Chapter Two

"Please Mum, don't cry any more." Andy looked across at his mother who sat on the settee dabbing at her red, tear swollen eyes with what was now twelve foot of wet scarf. "We'll find him, don't you worry," he said. Mrs. Winsborrow took a sip of tea from the cup that Karen held out to her.

"How can you find him you silly boy?" she wailed. "He's dead, your poor father's dead. Blown to bits by that . . . that crackpot contraption of his. Oh why did he have to start this inventing craze." Her face screwed up in anguish, her shoulders started to shake and then, burying her head once more in the soggy scarf, she went into another paroxysm of tears.

Andy looked across at his sister and shrugged hopelessly. Karen's eyes were also red rimmed from crying and Andy had been battling courageously to fight down the great lump in his throat that threatened to rise up and force him to burst into tears too. It was only the firm conviction that his father was still alive that stopped him from doing so. He gestured with his head to the door and Karen followed him outside.

"What are we going to do?" said Karen, when they were outside in the back garden. "I suppose we'll have to tell the police that Daddy has blown himself up."

"I don't think he has blown himself up," said Andy. He opened the side door into the garage, leaned against the door jamb and looked thoughtfully at the wreckage inside.

"Well? Go on Smartypants," said Karen. "Where is he then if he hasn't blown himself to bits?"

Andy turned round to face his sister. He had a faraway expression in his eyes and when he spoke it was with an air of certainty and conviction.

"I think his machine worked."

Karen stared at him. "You mean, you think he's gone back in time just like he said he would?"

"I think he's alive, I think his machine worked and that Dad has gone back in time and is now wandering about in the world as it was a hundred and twenty million years ago," said Andy.

"Oh, don't be so silly," spluttered Karen. "Daddy's inventions never worked, you know that. It's just not possible."

"Listen," said Andy. He sat his sister down on the old wooden box inside the garage then sat himself down on the workbench top. "I know that most of poor old Dad's inventions went wrong. We were always pulling his leg about it. But I think that perhaps this time he really did stumble onto something big, a really great idea, something that would do what he said it would and stagger the great scientists of the world. But as usual something went wrong. I think his mistake this time was he couldn't be bothered finding another three legs for his machine. The leg that the machine stood on was far too rickety and unsafe."

"But if what you say is true," said Karen. "How did he intend to get back from a hundred and twenty million years ago to the present time without his machine?"

"But don't you see, that's where the whole thing went wrong," said Andy, waving his arms in the air. "The machine was supposed to go back in time with him. If he had built it with four legs it would have worked perfectly, as it was, with that one silly leg, it was completely unstable. Everything was going smoothly until he slammed the door. The machine toppled off the bench and onto the floor. Something in the machine, some vital part, must have become dislodged with the impact of the fall and instead of both Dad and the machine going back in time, the machine stayed here and Dad was sent back to the dinosaurs on his own."

Karen looked even more forlorn. "Yes, I suppose we would have found some trace of him otherwise," she said. "But what are we going to do? Poor old Daddy with all those pterodactyls and dinosaurs. We'll never see him again." She sniffed and a great tear rolled down her cheek. Andy fished around in his pocket and produced a dark grey handkerchief with bits of chewing gum stuck to it. He held it out to Karen who decided it was better to wipe her eyes with her sleeve. They sat quietly for a while staring vacantly into space, each thinking the same thought. How were they going to get along without Dad? True, they had not seen very much of him when he was going through his inventing craze, but on the times that he was in their company he was great fun to be with. The thought of him being all alone with the great scaly monsters of prehistoric times and unable to escape to the present time filled them with dread. Perhaps he'd already been eaten. Suddenly Andy leaped up in the air waving his hands excitedly.

"I've got it!" he yelled, so loudly that his sister fell backwards off the box onto the garage floor.

"Got what? Got what?" she said, picking herself up and frowning at an oily patch that had appeared on her white socks.

But Andy didn't hear her. He was grovelling around on the floor, pushing pieces of machinery aside and collecting together all the bits of paper with scribbled notes on them, all the blueprinted plans and any other things written or drawn that he could find

"What are you doing?" said Karen.

"I've got it, I've got it, I've got it!" whooped Andy. He scooped the bundle of papers together and placed them on the workbench, then turned to face Karen with a triumphant gleam in his eye. "We're going to rescue him!"

"Rescue him? But how?"

"With these." Andy pointed to the pile of plans on the bench.

"But, but, I don't see . . ." spluttered the perplexed Karen.

"We are going to sort out all the plans and diagrams that Dad left and we're going to build another time machine following his drawings, but built with four legs instead of one, and then we're going to go back one hundred and twenty million years and rescue him."

Karen goggled at her brother as though he had gone mad. "But where shall we get all the bits and pieces?" she said at last.

"Well, quite a lot of the pieces are still here," said Andy, sweeping his arm round at the wreckage on the floor. "Some of it is a bit bent and some of it is beyond repair, so we'll have to make some new bits. We'll have to buy some electrical plugs and wire and a few bolts and nuts, but I bet if we try hard we could do it. What d'you think?"

"I can't see it working but I suppose it's the only hope we've got," she said. "But it will take ages. Daddy might have been eaten by now."

"Right!" said Andy. "So the sooner we start the better," and with that they both turned to the bench and with furrowed brows started to try and make sense out of the mass of figures and drawings on the blueprints in front of them.

"Heavens!" said Karen after a while. "This will take at least a fortnight."

Chapter Three

It took four months. During that time every spare moment was spent welding and soldering and hammering. Another bread bin lid disappeared from the house and another metal support to the car port was taken away and used. Carefully and meticulously they followed the plans and gradually the second time machine took shape.

Of course Mrs. Winsborrow had informed the police of her husband's disappearance and long delays to the making of the machine took place while three policemen came and looked over the garage. They were very suspicious and obviously didn't believe that Mr. Winsborrow had just vanished into thin air. They said that they would continue with their enquiries and giving Mrs. Winsborrow a cold hard stare they went away.

Mr. Winsborrow's employers had to be told too. He had worked at the bank in the town as a cashier. Mr. Prentice the bank manager called round to the house with a large bunch of flowers and some letters from the rest of the staff expressing their sorrow at the sad departing of a dear friend and colleague. This depressed the Winsborrow family terribly and after Mr. Prentice had gone there were more tears and the twenty foot scarf became all soggy again.

Eventually the day came when the last nut and bolt was fitted firmly into place. The children stood back and looked at their handiwork.

"It doesn't look the same as the one Dad built," said Karen doubtfully.

"That's only because we haven't painted it silver and we've used different bits here and there, but it should work in the same way," said Andy. "And it looks different with four legs instead of only one."

"I don't think we'd better tell Mum that we're going off to rescue Dad," said Karen. "She was so upset about him and we are all she's got left. She'd be worried sick if she thought there was a chance that the same could happen to us."

"I'm worried sick that it could happen to us too," said Andy.

"You're not going to get all scared and give up after all our hard work!"

"Don't be silly," said Andy. "But I must admit, I am nervous, my tummy's full of butterflies."

"Mine too," said Karen. "But come on, think, what're we going to do about Mum?"

"We'll leave a note," said Andy.

So they wrote a note which said

"Dear Mum, Please don't be cross with us and try not to worry, but we have rebuilt Dad's time machine and we are going in it to rescue him. We don't know when we shall be back, but we will be all right. Please don't get all worried. We love you.
Karen and Andy
P.S. We have got your bread bin lid."

They pinned the note onto Mrs. Winsborrow's knitting basket where she was sure to see it, then went into the kitchen and packed a large basket full of ham sandwiches, apples, a jar of peanut butter (Karen's favourite) and a packet of Rice Crispies (Andy's favourite), a flask of tea and a bottle of lemonade. This was Karen's idea. Ever practical she thought it wise to take plenty of provisions in case food was in short supply all those millions of years ago. They also took a torch, Mother's twenty-five foot scarf in case it was cold, and Mr. Winsborrow's pipe, baccy and matches, which they felt sure he would want if they managed to find him. Then after a last longing look around the house they climbed into the time machine.

They pushed the little plugs into their ears and pulled the studded seat belt around their chests and clicked it into the socket on the wall. Andy adjusted the dial on the panel to the setting marked "120 million years" then turned to his sister, his teeth chattering nervously and said, "All set?"

"Are you sure we followed Daddy's plans carefully enough?" asked Karen. She too was slightly ashen faced and she chewed anxiously at her lower lip.

"I've checked every nut and screw," said Andy. "And I'm as certain as I can be that we haven't missed anything out."

"But what if we blow up like Daddy did? I tell you what, let's phone up the police or the fire brigade, tell them where Daddy is, and let them go and rescue him. I mean, after all, that is their job." Her heart was thumping painfully against her ribs now that the time for the off had come. She felt at that moment that she would rather be anywhere else on earth rather than stuck in this silly time contraption that might disintegrate at the touch of a switch, blowing them both to kingdom come.

Andy looked at her wide eyed and she turned her face away ashamed and annoyed with herself for being babyish and trying to back down. She took a deep breath and turned back to face her brother.

"Well okay," said Andy, "I'll give the fire brigade a ring and . . ."

"Push the switch!" said Karen.

"What? Oh? All right," said Andy

And he did.

Chapter Four

They heard the whine of the motor under the seat increase in volume until it became a shriek that almost burst their eardrums. The green and red lights on the panel flashed on and off at a tremendous speed and the whole machine started to buck and shake like a bull at a rodeo. They experienced a strange kind of sinking feeling deep down in their stomachs. Like being in a lift plunging down a lift shaft.

Suddenly the little panel of glass that they were looking through into the garage went black. Andy turned to Karen whose face was lit up by the green and red lights from the panel.

"Looks like the light bulb in the garage must have blown," he shouted above the din.

"It doesn't matter," she yelled back. "We can still see."

Just then the violent lurching of the machine started to slow down and so too did the flashing bulbs. Below the seat the engine started to splutter and choke. The children stared at each other anxiously. It was just like being in a car that was running out of petrol. The machine gave three violent lurches then stopped completely. The lights went out on the panel and they were left in complete darkness.

"Well, that's a fat lot of good," said Karen from the blackness. "I told you that we hadn't checked the machine thoroughly enough."

"It's probably only a fuse gone or something," said Andy.

"Oh let's face it," said Karen. "We'll never be able to find Daddy. We've made the machine all wrong, there must be some bit that we've forgotten to put on."

"Don't give in," said Andy. "Like I said, I bet it's only a fuse or a wire that's become disconnected. I'll get out and have a look at the electrical circuit. Shan't be a tick."

He undid the seat belt, removed the ear plugs, opened the door and walked straight into a tree.

Karen heard the thump and then a yell as Andy fell. She grabbed the torch from the basket and pointed the beam of light through the open door. She gave a cry of astonishment. Just outside the door where minutes before had been their garage was the most enormous tree that she had ever seen. Andy appeared in the doorway tenderly rubbing his bruised forehead.

"Where did that come from?" said Karen pointing at the tree with a trembling finger.

Andy looked up at the great red-coloured tree trunk in amazement. He reached out and touched it. The bark was extremely soft and fibrous like the bearded part of a coconut. He pulled a piece off and crumbled it between his fingers. He turned round to Karen again, his eyes like saucers in the torchlight.

"I think we're here," he whispered.

"Here?"

"The machine worked. We're here!"

Karen climbed carefully out of the machine. They were standing knee-deep in wet grass. The ground felt

26

very soft and spongy and a few drips of water fell down on them from somewhere above their heads. She walked carefully round the tree closely followed by Andy who with an unexpected show of affection took hold of his sister's hand and held on to it tightly.

The tree really was huge. It must easily have been as big around the base as their house at home. Karen held the torch at arm's length. The beam flickered across the dark looming shapes of many more huge trees. The vegetation was thick and luxurious. Large, strangely shaped green leaves glistened wetly all around and here and there flashes of brilliant colour were picked out by the torch beam. Huge flowers hung bell-like from thick tangled stems that twisted like bind weed around the great gnarled tree trunks and from every quarter there came the steady drip drip sound of water falling from the branches onto the marshy grass.

The children stared out into the eerie stillness. They both felt the cold prickle of fear that comes when faced with the unknown. It was so quiet. The woods and forests of the twentieth century were always so full of life. It was only last summer that they had camped for a week in the New Forest with their parents and had woken at midnight to the loud screeching of an owl. They had lain fuzzy with sleep in their little blue tent listening to the noises of the night. The scurrying and scampering and scratching and calling of countless nocturnal creatures all fresh from sleep and ready to spend until the dawn hunting or being hunted.

But here it was different. Not a sound came from this primeval forest save the soft plop of water onto the wet, warm ground or the faint excited noise of their own breathing.

Suddenly both children stiffened with fear. Far away and almost so quietly that it was easy to dismiss as pure imagination there came a sound. They listened intently, gripping each other's hands tightly. Yes, there it was again, only slightly louder this time. A soft rustling followed by a dull thud. It got louder, something was coming their way, only the rustling was now changing into a louder and more frightening crashing sound. A sound of bushes being torn out by the roots and of trees creaking and crashing and splintering, and worst of all a grunting snarling noise that was deep and resonant and shook the whole forest until the tree trunks trembled and the drips of water which fell from the branches became a short, sharp torrential downpour.

With one accord the children turned and fled back into the time machine. They slammed the door behind them and sat huddled together trembling with fear on the wooden seat. The noise was deafening. All around they could hear the creaking and snapping and crashing of trees. The ground trembled and a great rumbling, grunting and roaring which sounded like a thousand express trains rushing through a tunnel, made their tinny vehicle rattle and threaten to shake itself to pieces. Something heavy fell against the side of the machine. It lurched over sideways at an impossible angle but didn't quite fall over.

"Let's get out of here!" yelled Karen, and started frantically pressing buttons and pushing levers.

"Wait! Wait!" Andy grabbed her arm. She struggled against him.

"Let me go" she screamed. "We'll get killed!"

But Andy put his arms across the panel of switches so that she couldn't get at them.

29

"Listen!" he bellowed. "It's going away!"

Karen stopped struggling and listened. Sure enough the crashing noise was going away from them now. Whatever it was must have passed within a few feet of where they were sitting. They stayed very still listening intently. Gradually the noise faded off into the distance and then there was silence.

"Phew! What on earth was that," said Andy, slumping back on the seat.

"I don't know, but it must've been enormous," said Karen. "Oh, come on, let's go back home. I don't like it here."

"We're not going home till we've found Daddy," said Andy firmly. "We've been working for the last four months on this and we're not giving in now!"

He leaned forward and readjusted the levers and dials back to the positions that they had been in before his sister's panic.

"You old silly," he said warmly. "If you had carried on fiddling with all the instruments, goodness knows where we would've ended up."

Karen grinned sheepishly and pushed the hair back out of her eyes.

"I'm sorry," she said and then, "Do you think we should stay where we are in the machine until it becomes light?"

"Good idea," said Andy. "It would be safest."

They made themselves as comfortable as was possible on the hard wooden bench. The machine was still tipped crazily at quite a steep angle and so it was extremely difficult to sit without one of them sliding down and squashing the other. But they managed, and gradually the time slipped by and the inky blackness that enveloped them dissolved into the soft greyness of early morning.

The children tumbled out onto the wet grass and gazed with renewed wonder at their surroundings. In the torchlight of the previous night there had been a solid inpenetrable forest. The scene now was one of complete devastation. The forest was still there, of course, but now a great path had been forced through the trees from left to right and as far as the eye could see. Huge trees had been torn from the earth and scattered like dandelions on all sides. The tree that they had been standing beside last night now lay on its side, its gigantic roots still clinging to a great ball of earth like a giant kelly doll that wouldn't stand up again. A big branch had fallen on top of the time machine and pinned it against the trunk of the tree. Andy immediately started to pull and heave at the branch. It toppled to one side with a crash. He then dropped down on to his hands and knees and began to peer at the ground intently.

"What on earth are you doing?" said Karen.

"Help me," said Andy. "The machine has been pushed at least a yard or two from its original position by that branch. It's important that we put it in the exact position it was in last night."

"What difference does it make?"

"It makes a lot of difference," said Andy, his nose still hovering over the ground. "If we get into the machine where it is now when it's time to go home we might end up half way through our garage wall."

"Ugh!" said Karen. "Nasty."

"Exactly," said Andy.

Eventually they found four indentations in the marshy ground made by the legs of the heavy time machine, and with much pushing and shoving they managed to get the machine back into its original position. They then carefully covered it with small branches and bits of bracken until it was completely hidden from view. This done they picked up the shopping basket with the food in it, sat down on a tree root and ate a hearty breakfast. Surprisingly the tea in the flask was still warm and the ham sandwiches were delicious.

"Which way shall we go?" said Andy, pointing at the tree strewn path.

"I reckon we ought to go in the opposite direction to the monster or whatever it was," said Karen. "I don't want to meet him again."

"Nor me," said Andy. He stood up and brushed the crumbs off his trousers. "Are you ready?"

Karen held out her hand and he pulled her to her feet. She glanced up and down the lane, swallowed hard and said "I'm ready."

"Right," said Andy. "Let's go and find Dad." He lifted the basket and they started off down the path, picking their way between the uprooted trees.

Chapter Five

It was hard going. Everywhere great gouts of earth had been pulled out of the ground leaving deep, ragged hollows that had to be climbed down into or around. Tangled roots tugged at their clothes and many of the mighty trunks that had to be climbed over had rough and jagged barks that scraped the skin from their knees. Nevertheless it was a fascinating trip. The foliage was completely different to any that they had ever seen before. Small bushes grew thickly at the feet of the big trees and from between their dark, shiny green leaves there gushed a profusion of flowers with dazzling colours. Immense clusters of pale red fruit hung from vines that twisted up and up around the tree trunks to the bright blue slit of sky above. The thick heady scent of grass and pollen and flowers hung almost visibly in the air around them. The ground was still very wet and spongy, but strangely warm. Perhaps only a very thin crust of the earth had cooled at this time, Karen thought to herself, and shuddered as the thought occurred to her that maybe inches below the thick, mushy carpet that she was now walking on, there bubbled the white hot core of the earth.

After two hours walking, the children found themselves on the edge of a vast rocky plain. Not a scrap of vegetation was to be seen. The forest had ended abruptly. It was uncanny, almost as though some giant hand had shaved a few thousand acres of the ground clean. To the left and to the right of them the edge of the forest stretched tall and true and ruler straight to the horizon. But to the front was this great sandy yellow plain. The air seemed lighter here after the oppressive heaviness of the forest. There was something terribly eerie about the place. Maybe it was the silence and complete stillness – nothing moved. It had been quiet in the forest. But within the forest the lack of sound had not been so sinister, protected as they had been by the trees and the warm beauty of the flowers. Now it seemed they had reached a dead place. A place where the silence sent a prickle of fear down the spine. It was a bit like watching television in a dark room of an empty house with the sound turned off. About four hundred yards away the flat yellow ground rose up sharply into a jumble of rocks which clustered around the base of a long low hill. It reminded Andy of a rounded piece of cheese. It was full of holes. All kinds of differently shaped holes. Some big, some small.

"Gosh," said Andy. "Have you ever seen so many caves?"

Sure enough large holes like moon craters were dotted around at the foot of the porous hill.

Andy flopped forward onto his stomach, cupped his chin in his hands and groaned loudly. A second later a louder groan echoed back to him across the flat ground. It was so loud it made his hair stand on end with fright and both children leapt panic stricken behind the nearest tree. They stood with their backs to the tree, hearts pumping loudly, not daring to move. Eventually Karen popped her head timidly round the tree again and said "I wonder what that was?" Immediately a booming voice answered back "*I wonder what that was.*"

Andy's shoulders relaxed and he threw his head back and laughed.

"Well, aren't we a couple of scaredies? It's only an echo," he said.

"*Only an echo!*" yelled the voice.

"Cooeee," shouted Karen.

"*Cooee!*" came the answer.

"Who's a big fatty?"

"*Who's a big fatty?*"

"Yaaaagh!"

"*YAAAAGH!*"

"Hello Bignose. How's your mother off for treacle pudding?"

"*FINE THANKS, HOW'S YOURS?*"

The children stood in stunned silence. That was not the answer an echo was supposed to give. Karen slowly eased her way behind the tree again. Andy was just about to follow her when something made him stop. For a second he thought he saw a tiny movement near one of the caves. Yes, there it was again, a small splash of colour against the yellow backcloth of the hill.

The tiny speck danced about from rock to rock, pale blue like faded denim. Andy rubbed his eyes and stared hard. Behind the moving object at the entrance to one of the caves some more splashes of colour fluttered and danced impossibly in mid-air. They jerked and pranced in unabandoned unison. A long line . . . something familiar . . . a washing line. Yes, it was a washing line. And the single moving object . . . a little more distinct now . . . arms, legs, waving ... something about the stoop of the shoulders ... that long gangling run ... leaping from rock to rock ... yelling ... that voice. The children rushed forward. "DADDY!" they cried. "Daddy! Daddy!" Stumbling over the sandy plain ... hearts in roofs of chests ... tears running down cheeks ... Daddy! Running over the great expanse of flat yellow ground that never seemed to decrease in width, pale blue denim clad figure waving and yelling ... "Get back, get back!" ... What does he mean? ... Half way there ... Screaming blue figure, "Get back, Get back to the trees" ... soft swishing sound ... flurry of giant wings and suddenly two great clawed feet clamped painfully around their chests and they felt themselves plucked up into the air, stomachs plummeting downwards, hearts stuffed high in their throats, stifling the screams.

Way down below they caught a glimpse of their father crouched down beside a rock, his head in his hands. Then trees blurred by, then clouds, and then ... they passed out.

Chapter Six

Karen woke up first. She had been dreaming, dreaming that she was falling from a very high height but never reaching the ground, so that the sickening feeling of having her stomach way up in her chest and not being able to breathe was with her all the time. The sun shone through her eyelids and her chest hurt. A strange grating noise which came from somewhere nearby set her teeth on edge and something hard and sharp was digging painfully into the small of her back. She turned her head away from the glare of the sun and slowly opened her eyes. A great wall of untidy branches and twigs was all that she could see.

She turned her head again and looked the other way. Beside her lay her brother, face downwards, his head cradled in his arms and behind him was a neat pile of large, orange spotted footballs. No, wait – they were the wrong shape to be footballs ... too long. Eggs, that's right, they were enormous eggs. Suddenly she remembered the great claws that had snatched them up and the savage beating of wings. So they were in a nest, a gigantic nest. Slowly she rolled over on to her stomach and looked behind her.

Perched on a rock beside the nest was a hideous bird-like creature. It had enormous bat-like wings and

a long snout with rows of slightly green but sharp looking teeth. It had very deep sunken blood red eyes
which seemed to be in a fixed position within the
leathery sockets. To look in a different direction it had
to move its whole head. Karen judged that it must be
at least eight feet tall. Untidy tussocks of gingerish
coloured hair sprouted here and there from the grey
porridge textured body, gradually merging with the
blacker hair which was at its thickest by the creature's
legs. The enormous, scaly three-toed claws clinging
firmly to the large rock looked as though they could
crush it to powder in a second.

A picture of a creature similar to this one was in one
of Karen's school books at home. Now what was it
called? A ptero . . . a pterodactyl. Yes, that was the
name, terribly hard to spell. She shuddered and
peered through the gaps in the floor of the nest. Far,
far below she could see the rocky ground and a river
slithering and glittering like a snake through trees and
boulders and disappearing into the edge of the forest a
bit further off.

The nest appeared to be built on a ledge half way up
a sheer cliff face. No escape that way. She looked up
and saw the other half of the cliff towering above her,
touching the little puffy clouds that drifted across the
hot sky.

The strange grating noise that Karen had first heard
when she woke up started off again. She looked over at
the pterodactyl. It had its back to her and its mouth
wide open. It moved its head back and forth and the
terrifying greeny white teeth grated and screeched
against the grey granite wall of the cliff.

She moved closer to her brother, her stomach
muscles tightening with fear.

"Sssh!" he whispered urgently through clenched teeth. "Don't make a sound."

"I thought you were still unconscious," she said, surprised "Oh, Andy, I think she's ... she's ...."

"Yes, I know," Andy interrupted. "She's sharpening her teeth."

"To eat us!" Karen moaned softly. "What're we going to do?"

Andy struggled hopelessly and buried his face in the twigs.

Just then the grating noise stopped. Both heads swung round to look at the reptile. The huge leathery face swung round to look at them. It had the strangest eyes the children had ever seen. Evil eyes. They were almost completely blood red. The pupils were long horizontal yellow slits and they lay deep in the dark parchment coloured leather sockets unmoving and hypnotic. It was difficult to look away from the penetrating stare of those eyes. The beast hunched up its wings and pulled its long neck down onto its shoulders. It shuffled towards them like an enormous and hideous old man, giving little sharp noises of pleasure. 'YAAAK! YAAAK! YAAK!' it went.

It turned to Karen first. She felt its hot foetid breath on her face. Its great snout opened up into an enormous wet, glistening cavern. Large droplets of saliva splashed down onto her legs and dress. She covered her face with her hands and waited for the end.

"Get out of that, you scaly brute!" She opened her eyes in surprise. It was Andy. He was clinging desperately to the monster's neck like a jockey on a runaway horse. The pterodactyl was rearing high into the air, its eyes bulging furiously. Great muffled snorts and grunts burst out from beneath something long and woolly that was knotted around its snout.

"Good heavens," thought Karen. "Mummy's scarf!"

The pterodactyl clawed frantically at its face, trying to pull the scarf free.

"Don't just lie there. Help me," screamed Andy.

The reptile threw its head in the air, sending Andy flying outwards towards the chasm below. He clung desperately to the loose end of scarf and swung back towards the nest. Karen suddenly woke from her petrified state. She scrambled to her feet, bunched up her fist, and threw a tremendous punch at the pterodactyl's head. Unfortunately just at that moment Andy came swinging back in to the nest on the end of the scarf. Karen's fist landed with a resounding smack on his right eye and with a loud howl he landed flat on his back on the floor of the nest. The pterodactyl spread its great wings and flew with a mighty honking and muffled squawking out from the ledge. Away above their heads it hovered tearing at the scarf with its claws and sending large shredded lumps of wool down to the rocks below. All too soon the monster managed to pull the remains of the scarf from its nose. It turned its huge bulk towards the nest again and with a terrifying angry shriek plunged downwards towards them, its jaws gaping hungrily.

Karen looked frantically around the nest. Her eye fell on the cluster of orange spotted eggs. She stumbled over to them and heaved the top egg from the pile. It was surprisingly heavy. She staggered to the edge of the nest and pushed it over the side. The pterodactyl let out a horrified scream, changed direction abruptly, and zoomed downwards past the ledge like a rocket to save her precious egg. Miraculously she caught the egg

in her mouth just before it reached the rocks below.

Karen looked over her shoulder. Andy was sitting up rubbing his eye which had turned a delightful red and purple colour.

"Don't just lie there. Help me!" she yelled.

The pterodactyl had begun its ascent back to the nest. She tugged another egg from the pile and rolled it over the edge. Flying at speed upwards, the monster nearly turned itself inside out with its efforts to turn when the second egg passed it. Again she made an incredible catch in the nick of time. By this time two more eggs were on the way down, one from Andy and another from Karen.

Shrieking hysterically the pterodactyl looped the loop. She caught Andy's egg neatly with the last remaining space in her mouth, had an attempt at Karen's, fumbled it and the egg burst with a splatter of white and yellow right on top of her head, where the shell sat like a comical hat. Thick gouts of bright yellow yolk oozed down and over the creature's eyes. She flew round and round blindly, squawking and screeching, demented with rage, turning and zig-zagging crazily from the cliff wall, spreading yolk like a crop sprayer. She hovered, flapping and frantically beating her wings about two hundred yards away for a moment or two then flew at great speed slap, bang, straight into the side of the cliff. There was a loud crunching noise followed by an enormous GULP! as the pterodactyl swallowed her own eggs.

She fluttered back from the cliff, yolk dripping from her jaws, went suddenly rigid and fell like a fallen tree, completely unconscious, down, down, down, until with a splash she landed in the river below.

Chapter Seven

It was midday. The sky was now a harsh golden yellow
except for the sun which hung in the centre, white like
the open door of a furnace. The little fluffy clouds had
long since scurried over the horizon as though away
from the heat. The rocky face of the cliff sucked in the
hot rays of the sun and hoarded them until its surface
was almost impossible to touch.

A tiny patch of shadow was cast by the outer edge of
the nest, barely covering the two children huddled
together away from the glare. Andy had draped his
jacket between the branches of the nest, which helped
to create a little more shade, but it was still unbearably
hot. They were totally exhausted. They had been up
on the ledge now for over 24 hours. The fight with the
pterodactyl had weakened them enough, but having to
endure a long freezing cold night and then a blistering
hot morning had left them physically and emotionally
drained.

"Things are looking pretty bad for us," Andy
thought to himself gloomily. The flask of coffee and the
bottle of lemonade were now empty and it was some
hours since they had had anything to drink. He ran his
tongue over his lips and glanced over at his sister. She
seemed to be fast asleep. Her cardigan was pulled up

over her head to protect her from the sun and she lay pressed flat into the shadow breathing heavily. He leaned forward and brushed away two brightly coloured insects which buzzed irritatingly around her head. Since the pterodactyl had gone these small insects had increased in numbers. They were about the size of a common house bluebottle but they had kingfisher blue bodies and yellow wings and they stung. Both children were covered with small red itchy spots where the insects had settled. He swatted another one from his arm and frowned.

"If it wasn't for me none of this would've happened," he thought. "Why did I have to insist on building another machine and coming back to this terrible part of history?"

Their position looked hopeless. Here they were stuck miles up an unclimbable cliff, they didn't know which way to go to look for their father, and even if they found him they might not be able to locate the time machine again.

"Oh dear, if only we hadn't become unconscious when the pterodactyl picked us up," he thought. "Then we just might have a clue which way to go ... Oh, anyway what's the use? We'll never be able to get down off this ledge." He rolled over onto his back and shielded his eyes with his arm. "Well, there is one good thing about all this," he muttered to himself. "At least we know that Daddy did in fact travel back in time and that he is safe and well." THWOCK! "So if we could only get down from this rotten cliff," THWOCK! "I wonder ... now if we get all our clothes and tied them all together ..." THWOCK! "They just might reach down far enough for us to ..." THWOCK! Andy frowned. His train of thought was being interrupted. What on earth was that noise? THWOCK! Suddenly he was wide awake, his nerves jangling. Whatever that noise was, it sounded sinister. He pushed himself up onto his knees and peered over the edge of the nest. What he saw made his heart leap with fright. He shook Karen's shoulder roughly and her sleepy face emerged from beneath the cardigan.

"Um? Eh? Wassamatter? Is it breakfast time?" she mumbled.

Andy pointed downwards and she knelt up quickly and looked over the ledge.

Way down half way between the nest and the rocks below was a thing . . . a creature . . . the strangest creature the children had ever seen. It certainly was not in any history books that they knew of. It was about as big as a fully grown elephant and it did in fact have a trunk like an elephant except that it was much longer and completely pink and strangely translucent. The head was quite comical with two almost human ears on each side and big bright twinkling eyes. Just below the trunk was a small cupid bow mouth that was bright red and looked as though it was painted on by lipstick and from the mouth jutted two white and pointed teeth. The body looked completely round. An enormous ball of bright orange coloured hair. But strangest of all were the creature's feet. They were like large upside down soup bowls, black and shiny and stuck on the end of incredibly spindly legs. The animal was plodding very slowly up the vertical face of the cliff. With every step it took it would hold its foot to its mouth, shoot out a very long tongue and lick the sole thoroughly, then it would press the foot firmly against the rock face. This last action made a loud

THWOCK! noise.

"Prepare to repel boarders," yelled Karen. She stopped and picked up the last remaining pterodactyl's egg and staggered to the edge of the nest with it.

"Hang on, not yet," Andy held his arm out to stop her heaving the egg over the edge. "Wait until it's a bit nearer, you might miss."

So they balanced the egg on a stout branch and waited. THWOK! THWOK! THWOK! The curious creature plodded upwards licking its feet as it did so until at last it was only about two yards from the nest.

"Take aim," said Andy. "Steady, steady . . . right, FIRE!"

Karen pushed the egg and it plunged dead on target towards the strange creature's head. The little painted mouth suddenly became a gaping hole, the egg went in without touching the sides and disappeared like a bucket going down a well. There was a soft plopping noise and the mouth closed up again into its little rosebud smile. The creature was now level with the nest. The children, goggle-eyed, cringed against the back of the nest, sure that the end was now near. It leaned its huge body against the side of the nest and stretched out its long trunk towards Karen's face. She shut her eyes tight, too exhausted to fight any more and waited for the sharp teeth to sink into her flesh. Two soft lips touched her cheek. There was a long gurgling noise like a bath emptying followed by a wet popping noise. It was the sloppiest wettest kiss that she had ever received. She opened her eyes and stared at the creature in astonishment. It looked down at her, nodding its head, licking its lips and smiling at her in the most friendly fashion, and not in the least bit aggressively.

Andy still had his eyes squeezed shut and an agonised expression on his face. Karen nudged him in the ribs and pointed at the great beaming face that loomed over them.

"It kissed me," she said.

Andy didn't answer, he just stared up at the monster.

"It kissed me," Karen repeated.

The monster lifted its head and pointed the long translucent trunk straight upwards. The mouth opened and from it came forth a deep gravelly croaking noise.

"EEP EEP EEP BUNJEEEEEEEE"

It leaned forward again and gave Andy a juicy wet kiss on the forehead then threw its head back again and croaked even louder "WARRA WARRA WARRA EEP EEP BUNJEEEEEE!"

"I think it wants to be friendly," Karen whispered. She leaned forward tentatively and touched the creature's trunk.

"Hello," she said. "Er, good boy, good boy," as though she was addressing a dog.

The huge head turned to one side. It seemed to be listening attentively. It opened the small red mouth and once again the curious croaking voice came rumbling up from the cavernous depths of the great round body.

"EEP . . . EEP . . . GOO BOI" it boomed, again it gave her a wet kiss on the face.

"It *is* friendly," shouted Andy, and jumped to his feet with relief.

"EEP – EEP – WARRA WARRA FRENLEEE. FRENLEE. BUNJEEEEE," it said.

Andy patted the long trunk and smiled up at the big cheerful face. "You had us worried for a while. We thought we were going to get eaten."

"GO . . . GE . . . EEP . . . EEP . . . EETIN." It smiled and looked back and forward between the two children making little clucking noises at the back of its throat and looking as though it might start handing out more kisses at any moment.

"You're quite a mimic aren't you old chap?" said

Karen. "You sound as though you're trying to copy everything we say."

Andy nodded. "Yes, he's a bit like a huge hairy mynah bird."

"EEP ... EEP ... MINE A BIRD" the strange animal croaked.

"No, no," said Andy, "Mynah Bird."

"NOOO, NOOO MINA BURRRD," came the answer.

The children sat back in the nest and hooted with laughter. They roared, clutching their sides, tears streaming down their cheeks, allowing the tensions of the past few hours to flow out and away, happy to have met one creature at least that wasn't after them for food. In fact, so excited were they at meeting this friendly ball of orange hair, that all thoughts of their thirst and their predicament were temporarily forgotten.

The next fifteen minutes or so were spent saying words to the huge animal which he immediately mimicked. He seemed to relish each word, rolling it around his tongue before saying it and smiling happily when the children praised him for getting it right. The game went on and on, and surprisingly with each new word the big friendly creature's pronunciation became better and better. It became increasingly evident to Karen and Andy that here was no ordinary animal but an animal with a keen intelligence. At times when there was a lull in the flow of words and the children just sat quietly, he would lean forward and say anxiously "MORE" or even string two words that he had heard together and say "MOREPLEESE". He never left any gap between the words and said everything in a rush as though if he didn't get them out of his mouth quickly enough he would forget them.

It was quite extraordinary. After two more hours every word of conversation that passed between the two children was picked up and seemingly stored away in a filing cabinet up in the large hairy head. He retained everything. He put words together at first hesitantly and then with increasing confidence, like a good student of a foreign language. Occasionally he would throw his head in the air and let out the piercing "EEP EEEP EEP WARRA WARRA WARRA BUNJEEEEEE!" noise and then lean forward as though nothing had happened and say "WOTSDENEXTWORD?"

"This is fantastic." Andy scratched his head and looked at his sister. "If we had gone forward in time instead of backwards, I would have expected to discover a super intelligence. But we've travelled millions of years backwards in time, where all the creatures according to our teacher at school were supposed to be small brained. Gosh, won't we have something to tell them when we get back? This should alter the history books."

"THIS'LLOLTERDEHISTRYBOOKS," beamed the big hairy face.

"*If* we get back", said Karen dismally. "We're still no better off than when the pterodactyl brought us up here for her supper." She stood up and looked down at the terrifying drop to the rocks below.

At this their new friend wagged his trunk and looked from side to side, scanning the cliff wall quickly with his little eyes.

"WERESATERRYDAKTILDEN?" he said, a frown of concentration creasing his forehead.

"Pardon?" stammered Andy.

"I think he said 'Where's the Pterodactyl then?' "
said Karen.

"Oh," said Andy, speaking slowly, still unable to
believe that the creature could understand. "We
er . . . we threw eggs at it and it fell into the river."

The creature screwed up its eyes as it strived to work
out the meaning of Andy's words. It blinked twice,
then said "WARRAPITTEE, WARRAPITTEE."

"Oh dear," said Karen. "I'm sorry — was it your
friend?"

The huge hulk suddenly started shaking with
laughter until it looked as though it would shake its
suction cups loose and fall off the wall.

"TERRYDAKTILSDONTAVEFRENS,"   he
laughed, wiping a tear from his eye with the end of his
trunk.

"NONOEYEMENTWARRAPITTEEABOWT-
IT'S EGGS."

It took the children some time to work this last one
out, but at last they understood.

"Oh, I see," said Andy. "You like eating pterodactyl's eggs?"

"LUVUMLUVUM," was the reply. Its eyes closed
in rapture "YUMMYYUMMYYUMMEE."

"Oh dear. We're sorry if we've thrown away your
dinner. But we had to protect ourselves or we would've
been eaten."

"DUZENTMATTERDUZENTMATTER."   It
paused, searching for words, then "EEP EEP EEP . . .
PLENTYMORENESTSABOWT."

Andy groaned and held his stomach. "Oh please,
don't talk about food," he said. "I haven't eaten for so
long. I'm starving." He put his hands to his ears as the
creature suddenly shrieked "EEP EEP EEP WARRA

WARRA WARRA BUNJEEEEEEEEEEE!"

"I've got an idea," Karen said, her ears still ringing from the noise. She pointed over the edge of the nest at the ground far below, and speaking very slowly and clearly said "Do you think you could carry us down to the ground?"

The little eyes looked down in the direction of Karen's finger, then up to Karen's face, then across to Andy's face, then up at the cliff wall. A big smile spread across its face and it said "EEP EEP ... JUMPONABACK."

"Hang on a minute," Andy blurted out nervously. "Will your feet still stick to the wall with our combined weights?"

It put its head between its legs and looked at the ground again, then shook its head.

"NOTGONNACLYM – GONNAFLY."

"What to you mean?" said the children, suddenly afraid again. How could it fly? After all, the thing didn't have any wings. Maybe they hadn't heard properly.

"JUMPONABACK," the thing repeated.

"Well, what have we got to lose?" shrugged Andy, climbing over the edge of the nest and clinging to the bright orange hair on the creature's back. If we don't get off this ledge soon we'll starve anyway." Karen nodded and joined him, her eyes tight shut with fear.

"HEERWEGOW," it cried. "EEP EEP WARRA WARRA WARRA BUNJEEEEEEE!"

Suddenly it pointed its long trunk straight into the air. The snout tip closed up tight like a fist and the creature started to blow into its trunk. It started to swell bigger and bigger. The little mouth opened and shut sucking in great quantities of air and forcing it into the trunk. Soon above them the trunk was transformed into a massive balloon which looked as though it would burst at any moment. Little pink veins criss-crossed in a fine lattice work all over the ever swelling globe and the flesh had become so stretched that it had almost become transparent.

There were four soft popping noises as the great hairy animal detached its feet from the wall and then slowly they started to drift away from the ledge and out into space.

Once away from the ledge, the creature started to let small amounts of air escape from its trunk and gradually they started to descend. The air came out in a high pitched, spluttering shriek, making the same kind of noise that a balloon makes when the neck is pinched and stretched in the fingers.

It was a bit frightening at first. Andy started to worry that the thing might have loose hair and dandruff problems like his Father had and that he would plunge to his death clutching handfuls of hair. But his fear turned to excitement as they got lower and started to sweep in over the treetops like a helicopter. Down there he could see that the tiny little river that he had seen from the ledge was on closer inspection a raging torrent. The little bushes were huge thick conifers and the pebbles became enormous rocks. They floated down along the path of the river and landed gently on a mossy bank. The water at this point had formed a still pool and they were some way from the deafening roar of the main river.

"That was super," said Karen enthusiastically. "Thank you very much Mr. er, um – please what do we call you? What's your name?"

"EEP, EEP, AMABUNJEE," it said, its head bob-

53

bing up and down enthusiastically.

"AMABESTBUNJEEINAHOLEWORL."

"A Bunjee," said Andy. "What a lovely name. Are there other Bunjees near here?"

"NOAMAONLIBUNJEEINAWORL," it said.

"But there must be other Bunjees," said Karen, "You must have a mother or a father or sisters or brothers, you can't be the only one."

The Bunjee suddenly looked terribly sad. Its little bottom lip trembled slightly and a tear trickled from its eye and down its trunk.

"MAMOMMYGOTEETENBYATIRANASOR-AZ."

"Aaaw!" said the children sympathetically.

"MADADYBLEWHIMSELFUPTILLEBUST."

"Aaaw."

"MASISTAETTOOMANIEGGS."

"Aaaw."

"ANALLARESTGOTTAMEEZILSANDYED."

"Oh, what a shame," cried Karen. "All your relations gone just like that. No wonder they're not in the history books," she whispered to Andy.

"Will you excuse us a moment, Mr. Bunjee?" Andy croaked. "If I don't have a drink soon I'll dry up completely." He waded quickly into the pool of water. It felt so deliciously cool that he threw his arms up happily and let himself sprawl forward onto his face with a splash. Karen joined him and the Bunjee stood on the bank with a slightly puzzled expression as they drank and splashed and wallowed happily.

At least ten minutes went by before it said "DONTCHOOCAREABOUTDEPRANNAZ?"

"Pardon?" said Karen, standing up waist deep in the water.

"DEPRANNAZ," the Bunjee repeated.

Andy looked at his sister puzzled. "What does he mean? Prannaz?"

Karen said, "You don't mean PIRANHAS?"

"EEP, EEP — DASWOTEYESED," the Bunjee nodded. "PRANNAZ!"

One second later the children stood dripping beside the Bunjee on the bank and staring back horrified at the water. It had only been a week ago that they had been learning all about piranhas at school. How a shoal of the deadly little fish could strip a carcase to the bone in seconds.

Karen shuddered. "Why didn't you tell us?" she asked.

"NOBUDDYASKIDME," said the Bunjee.

Andy sat down with a squelch on the grass. "Everything is so dangerous in this age," he moaned. "I don't think we'll ever find Dad and get out of here alive." He looked up forlornly at the other two. "We've been lucky so far. Nearly trampled on by something as soon as we arrived here. Then picked up by a pterodactyl and rescued by dear old Bunjee here, and now just missing death by a hairsbreadth in a piranha infested river." He stared down at his feet in exasperation. "I haven't a clue what to do or where to look next."

The Bunjee nudged Karen with the end of its trunk. "HEY," it said. "WATTAMARRAWIDHIM?"

Karen smiled apologetically at Bunjee. "I'm sorry," she said. "You must think we're terribly rude. Perhaps we ought to put you completely in the picture and tell you the whole story."

So Bunjee licked his feet and stuck himself sideways on to a large boulder (where he said he was most comfortable) and Karen and Andy squatted below, their clothes steaming dry in the hot sunshine as they started to relate their story. Speaking as slowly as they could, trying not to use too many long words, they told him all about their father's inventions and the time machine going wrong and how they had built another one. How they had seen their father at the gruyere cheese looking desert. Of the pterodactyl picking them up and of the fight with the eggs. When they had finished Bunjee licked his feet again and started plodding around the side of the boulder thoughtfully. The little lips pursed and he whistled in a tuneless way, his brow creased in concentration and his feet THWOCKED hollowly with every step.

At last he stopped and looked down at the children. They looked up at him expectantly. "Well?" they said in unison. The Bunjee puffed himself up and he took a deep breath as though he was just about to start a long lecture and said, "AMHUNGRI!"

"Oh, that's a fat lot of help!" said Andy crossly.

"CANTFINKONNAEMTEESTUMAK," said Bunjee.

"I'm hungry too," wailed Karen. "Bungee, where can we find some food?" and then she added, "And I don't mean pterodactyl's eggs."

"FROOT?" asked Bunjee.

"Fruit would be super," said Karen.

Without another word Bunjee unplugged himself from the boulder, walked across the river bank and hopped sideways on to the cliff face, where he ambled slowly along about four feet from the ground. The children followed in silence.

After about an hour's walking they had covered a distance of approximately one mile. The Bunjee was infuriatingly slow and several times the children wandered on ahead and sat on a rock until he caught up. Eventually, however, after following the meandering line of the cliff for another half hour they turned a corner and were confronted by a wall of dense shrubbery. The trees were small and stunted with branches that were gnarled and twisted, but from the thick foliage hung a dazzling variety of the most succulent fruit the children had ever seen.

Great clusters of purple pear shaped fruit hung from sharply spiked branches on one tree, while from another brilliant yellow flowers spurted like small fountains from the sides of massive green globes that gushed sweet sticky juice when bitten into. Here and there the children could see more familiar fruits, apples, oranges and large yellow plums. But everything here was on a much larger scale and most of the plants were strange and unfamiliar to the children's eyes.

It was some time since the children had eaten and so they set to with a will, stuffing great handfuls of the fruit into their mouths, working from tree to tree experiencing each time a new taste. Calling to each other through overloaded mouths, "Hey, come and try this one, its's super," or "Look at the colour of this one, isn't it beautiful?"

The Bunjee meanwhile plodded slowly up the cliff towards a nest that he had spotted high above the trees. He stopped occasionally and looked back protectively at the children down below.

"STRANGEKREECHURES," he thought. "FANCYEETINFROOT!" He licked his feet and climbed a bit higher. "EGGSISMUCHNICER," he felt strangely happy. For the first time since his last relative died he had actually spoken to another living thing. He had tried mimicking and picking up the language of other creatures, but it was useless. None of the other animals could think. His earnest attempts at conversation had always been met by blank stares and grunts. It had been beyond his wildest dreams that there could be another type of animal, another species, that he could learn to have a stimulating conversation with. But here were these two strange creatures who had come from heaven knows where and some other time and they could actually think like he did. It was marvellous. Admittedly they did speak rather slowly, those strange gaps between words. But given time and a good elocution teacher like a Bunjee, they'd soon learn to speed up. He hummed a little tune to himself and edged nearer to the nest, wondering as he did so how he could help his new found friends.

Down in the prehistoric orchard below the children had almost eaten their fill. They lay on their backs at the foot of a tree and watched through half closed eyes the Bunjee high above on the cliff. Andy threw the core of a green melon sized apple into the long grass.

"That was the best meal I think I've ever had," he murmured.

"Me too," said Karen.

"What a pity they don't have fruit like that in the twentieth century."

"Mmm. Which fruit did you like the best?"

"The juicy blue ones," said Karen, "Definitely the blue ones. I've never tasted anything so delicious."

They lay contentedly for a moment or two saying nothing. Somewhere to the right of them a bird squawked and the little dot on the cliff picked up an egg from the nest with its trunk and popped it into its mouth. It was cool under the heavy green branches and the feast had made them feel drowsy. Andy shut his eyes and fell asleep. Karen plucked a long stem of grass and chewed at the cool yellow end. She too closed her eyes and having done so, missed by a fraction of a second the sudden movement in the foliage behind her.

This came from a plant which was slightly taller than the rest of the bushes around. The children had ignored it when they were eating because it did not appear to bear any edible fruit. Perhaps another reason was that it was an extremely ugly plant compared with the others. It was shaped like the trumpet part of a daffodil, but about seven feet tall and dark green in colour. There were no leaves, no stem, no fruit – just a plain, dark green trumpet, sticking solidly out of the ground and pointing its open end at the sky. At least this is how it looked when the children had been awake. Now a change was taking place. From the centre of the trumpet there arose six glistening black tendrils. On the end of each tendril was a brown leathery pod. They climbed slowly out of the main stem of the plant like monstrous worms. With a soft popping noise the pods burst open and from the centre of each cascaded a mass of sticky white tubes which writhed like living spaghetti through the grass towards the sleeping children. The first sticky tube fastened itself tightly around Karen's ankle. She awoke immediately, but her horrified scream was cut off by another white worm which flopped revoltingly across her mouth. She struggled violently but another fat white tube pinned her arms to her sides, another wound around her legs and soon she was wrapped in an enormous cocoon of white stickiness which squeezed her in such a tight grip that she could hardly breathe. The tubes were quickly pulled back towards the leathery pods. Karen was lifted high into the air until she could look down into the hollow trumpet of the plant. She caught a glimpse of dark red hairs growing wetly from the sides, the black pit of the bottom like an open throat, and then with a grotesque sucking noise she felt herself being pulled down into the darkness.

Chapter Eight

Bunjee stood motionless beside the nest, high on the cliff wall. He felt decidedly odd. A strange rumbling was taking place in his stomach. He rolled his eyes around his head and licked his lips unhappily. He felt nauseated. He glanced at the six remaining eggs in the nest. They lay in their usual neat pile and normally he would have gobbled them up in seconds but there was something wrong. The egg that he had just swallowed lay heavily and uneasily inside him and he wanted to be sick. He leaned over, picked another egg from the nest and cracked it open on a sharp edge of rock. Immediately he knew why he felt sick. The egg was rotten. A foul stench escaped from the broken shell and what should have been yellow yolk oozed greenly out and splattered on the rock. He screwed up his face in an expression of disgust and let the putrid egg fall to the ground below.

"UGGG!" he mumbled, almost in tears. "AVEEETIDAROTTIDEGG!" He was annoyed with himself for not noticing that the nest had been abandoned. All the signs were there. Small pieces of rock that had fallen from the cliff lay in the bottom and the whole nest was in a state of disrepair. It looked as though it had been abandoned for at least six months. But greedily and unthinkingly he had just stuffed one of the eggs into his mouth as soon as he had reached the nest.

"EEP, EEP, OWDRATANBOVVERASHUN!" he fumed. "AMASTOOPIDBUNJEE."

He wished now that he was a bit more like his two new found friends and could eat fruit instead of having to climb laboriously up cliffs hunting for eggs.

He glanced downwards to see how they were getting on. He could see Andy lying asleep at the foot of a tree. Karen he thought must still be eating. But where was she? He should be able to see her from here. To one side of the wood the river gurgled and glinted as it wound its way between the rocks and disappeared behind a high hill far in the distance. The only other sign of movement was from the tops of the trees as they swayed gently in the soft breeze that wafted along the valley. He screwed his eyes up, straining to see between the leaves and branches far below. Something white moved to one side of the sleeping boy.

"AHTHERSHEIZ," thought Bunjee, relieved. Then he noticed that the white thing had long strings attached and that it was being dragged along the ground. He watched horrified as the whole tangled mass suddenly whisked up into the air and disappeared into the dark centre of a sinister dull green plant.

"OHKRIKEY!" wailed Bunjee, nearly falling off the cliff with fright. "ITSABLUDSUCKAPLANT." Of all the dangers that were present in those prehistoric times the thing that frightened Bunjee most was the bloodsucker plant. Two of his relatives had fallen victim to its sticky tentacles in the past and his mother had always warned him not to go near strange plants.

"ANDY!" he screamed. "ANDYANDYANDY!"

Andy woke up and gave the Bunjee a cheerful wave.

"ITSABLUDSUCKAPLANT!" shouted Bunjee. "KARENSINABLUDSUCKAPLANT!" Andy waved up at him again and went back to sleep.

Bunjee groaned loudly. What on earth was he to do. He was very frightened of the bloodsucker plant but he couldn't just stand by and do nothing. Maybe he was too late already and Karen was already dead. He looked around frantically for something to throw. Suddenly he remembered how the children had saved themselves from the pterodactyl and an idea occurred to him, an absurd idea, a crazy idea, but one which just might work. He leapt off the wall and into the nest. He sat down and gave his feet a thorough licking and then carefully, so as not to break them, he stuck an egg on to each foot. Quickly he inflated his trunk, squirmed over the edge of the nest, and floated out into space, releasing air at the same time and descending rapidly. By moving the tip of his trunk around he was able to steer himself in the direction that he wanted and seconds later was zooming in diagonally towards the great trumpet shaped plant. He was terribly frightened. At any second he expected the dreadful white tentacles to reach out of the green trumpet and envelop him. But he gritted his teeth and rushed onwards. When he was within a few feet of the plant he took an enormous breath and re-inflated his trunk. This almost brought him to a halt and he dangled about twenty feet above the gaping mouth. With pounding heart he looked down. He could see the wet red hairs on the throat of the plant, darkening deeper down until they disappeared into blackness. There was no sign of Karen and his face creased with agony

at the thought that he might be too late. He stuck his legs out at right angles to his body and then brought them together with all his strength. The eggs smashed together and the putrid green yolk poured out and down the gullet of the plant. The smell of four six-month-old pterodactyl eggs was unbelievable. Bunjee deflated his trunk with one last snort like an untied balloon that had just been released, and zig zagged off until he landed in the top of a tree. Winded, he scrambled through the foliage and peeked out anxiously at the bloodsucker plant.

For a long time nothing happened. The great trumpet stood green, unmoving and formidable. Then from somewhere way down in the dark regions of its digestive system there came a deep gurgle. A kind of coughing sound like a very old man clearing his throat. The plant started to jerk convulsively. Suddenly it seemed to stoop lower, its middle part bellied out, another loud throaty gurgle and then it sprang back into place and spat. The loudest spitting noise you could imagine. From the mouth shot a great stream of foul smelling egg, two small furry animals, and Karen. She sailed up into the air, her face screwed up in an expression of disgust. She did two somersaults and landed with a bump right on top of Andy.

Andy jerked upright, his eyes starting from his head, and for a moment or two neither said a word, Karen because she was too astonished at ever seeing the outside world again, and Andy because all the breath had been knocked out of him. But at last after much gasping and puffing he managed to yell indignantly "What on earth are you doing, you great fathead?"

Karen was still in a state of shock and promptly burst into tears.

"Phew! You smell awful!" Andy pulled himself out from under her wet body and held his nose in disgust. Karen wailed even louder. She got to her feet and staggered away from the small wood. Andy followed still holding his nose. When she was sure that she was well out of reach of the plant she fell to her knees, put her head in her hands, and howled. It was such a relief to find herself still alive. She was wet through, horribly sticky and Andy was right, she did smell awful. It was also a relief after all the tensions of the past few hours to have a really good weep and get it out of her system.

Andy stood a few feet away, utterly perplexed. He just couldn't understand it. He wanted to comfort his sister but the smell wouldn't let him get close enough. He was aware that he smelt pretty badly too. His shirt was saturated where Karen had landed on him. It was very confusing. He wished that she would stop crying and explain what had happened.

Just then he felt a soft tap on the shoulder. Bunjee stood behind him wearing a worried expression.

"ISHEEGONNABEAWRITE?" he asked.

"Bunjee, thank goodness you're here," Andy said. "Have you any idea what's going on?"

Bunjee looked extremely distressed. He was shaking all over. It was the closest he'd ever been to a blood sucker plant and perhaps the only brave thing he'd ever done in his life.

"FANKEVANSHEESALRITE," he said.

"But what's happened?" said Andy in exasperation. There was no answer. Bunjee had fainted.

Chapter Nine

"Well, they didn't take long to dry," said Karen, struggling back into her clothes. She popped her head out from behind the large rock where she had been dressing and gave the other two a broad smile. "It's only five minutes since I washed my clothes and hung them out and the sun has dried them already." She walked towards them, running her fingers through her hair in an attempt to get some of the tangles out.

Andy sat on the grass in his underpants. He leaned over and touched his clothing which lay spread out beside him. Everything was dry so he stood up and started to dress.

"Bunjee has just told me the whole horrible story," he said.

Karen shuddered. "I'd rather forget all about it," she said. "I've never been so scared. It was terrifying."

"And to think I slept through the whole thing." Andy shook his head, then looked up at Bunjee. "Bunjee, you were very, very brave."

Bunjee went slightly pink, looked down at his suction cups and said "AWITWUZNOTHIN".

"You were marvellous," said Karen. She patted Bunjee affectionately on the back. "Are you feeling any better? Or do you still feel sick?"

Bunjee shrugged. "WELLAHDONTFEELUNG-RYENNYMORE," he said.

"Well, if you are not thinking of your tummy any more, can you think what we are going to do about rescuing our father?"

"IVETHUNK," said Bunjee.

"Yes?" chorused the children, staring at him hopefully.

"EYEFINK," said Bunjee, "EYEKNOWWEAR-DESANDYPLACEIZ."

"Pardon?" said Andy.

"He thinks he knows where the sandy place is," said Karen.

"Is it a place full of big holes in the ground and lots of caves everywhere?"

Bunjee nodded. "EYEFINKSO." He sat back, scratched his head reflectively with the tip of his trunk, and told the children that many years ago when he was very young there were lots and lots of Bunjees in the world. (At least a dozen, he said.) He had lived with his mother and father and all the other Bunjees in a huge cave set in the side of a hill. They had been very happy there. They took it in turns to go hunting for eggs and at night they all hung together upside down from the roof of the cave, chatting and huddled together for warmth. The days were spent playing games. Racing up the cliff was a favourite. He remembered holding the Bunjee record for a while, racing at breakneck speed up a sixty foot cliff and back down again in only three hours and twenty minutes. He smiled proudly down at the children and they made appreciative polite noises, like "Oh yes, very good", and "My goodness, what speed!" and then he continued his tale.

They had all felt fairly secure in the cave. The entrance had been protected by a fall of rock and shingle, so any animal that ventured too close to the cave always made quite a noise. When this natural alarm signal went off the Bunjees would simply climb to the roof of the cave, which was very high, and hang there out of reach of any predator until it got frustrated and went away. Everything was fine. Everybody was happy and the days came and went in an idyllic fashion. He was responsible for helping the younger Bunjees with their studies. Trunk inflation and deflation, how to land properly, foot licking lessons, the timing of egg raids. When pterodactyls were usually to be found off their nests, and important things like that.

But one evening, one never to be forgotten evening, when they were all feeling fairly tired after a day's playing and eating, a terrible thing happened. The clatter of loose rocks outside gave the alarm and as usual they plodded up the sides of the cave, taking care that the children's feet were well licked and helping old Grandfather Bunjee who had difficulty unplugging his feet from the walls when he walked. They hung upside down in the darkness and watched the cave entrance curiously, expecting perhaps a sabre toothed tiger or a long toed grummett snapper. (The children looked puzzled, but didn't like to interrupt to ask what a long toed grummett snapper was.) The clattering of the rocks outside got noisier and noisier. Suddenly there was a terrifying roar and a huge clawed arm reached in and tore the rocks away from the mouth of the cave. It was a tyrannosaurus! The huge head cut out the light almost completely. It reached in as far as it could with its arm. Grandad was so frightened that his feet dried up and he fell off the roof and landed on his head down below. The Monster grabbed one of the Bunjees. We couldn't see which one of us it was at first, and with a great snorting he went away.

"Oh, how terrible, Bunjee," said Karen, "Was it your mother?"

Bunjee nodded sadly. There was a long pause. The children looked down at the ground, not knowing what to say. Bunjee took a deep breath and continued his story.

After the tyrannosaurus had gone there was total chaos in the cave. Terrified children had to be calmed down, Bunjee himself had to be consoled, and poor Grandad Bunjee had a lump on his head the size of a coconut. Bunjee's father took control of the situation. When everybody had calmed down he warned them that now that the monster had discovered their home, he would be back. They would have to move out and find somewhere else to stay. Had anyone any ideas about where they could go? Bunjee's Uncle put up his trunk and everyone stopped talking and waited for him to speak. Uncle had always been a bit of a roamer. On food expeditions he invariably went miles further than anyone else. The other Bunjees never strayed more than a mile or so from the cave, but Uncle always liked to wander off into unexplored territory, sometimes staying away for days. There had been times when the Bunjees had given him up for lost but he had always reappeared and usually laden with eggs.

He told the others that on one of his trips he had come across a sandy desert that was filled with holes and caves and that it looked an ideal place for Bunjees to live. But it was a long way away and they would have to travel by way of the river.

Bunjee himself had been so unhappy about losing

his mother that he couldn't remember much about the trip. A few things came back to him. He remembered that they had all been very frightened. Someone had found a large log, and he remembered being squashed up on it and floating very quickly down the river between great rocks, of how they had capsized once,

and two Bunjees had been drowned. Of a very nasty creature with great scales on its back wading into the water and attacking them, which accounted for three more of their number, and how they had escaped by running into the woods. They never actually reached the sandy place with the caves, but decided to settle in the wood near a large cliff that seemed to have an abundance of pterodactyls' nests on its ledges. Sadly, Bunjee finished his story by telling of his father over-inflating his trunk one day in a temper and popping like a balloon, of his sister over-eating and then of the dreadful measles epidemic that saw off the rest of his species. When he had finished he sat looking so forlorn that the children could find no words to say. Both moved closer to him, wrapping their arms around him, as far as that was possible on his fat body, and Andy pulled out his grubby handkerchief to wipe away a tear that suddenly trickled down Bunjee's trunk.

They stood like that for a long time, each staring into space, lost in their own thoughts. The children had grown to be extremely fond of the Bunjee. His was a harrowing tale. What a pity that such nice creatures were doomed to die out. It seemed such a shame that there were so many savage animals around that would survive a few million or so more years and yet a kind goodnatured species like the Bunjee should be on the brink of extinction.

Bunjee suddenly stood up and shook himself out of his trance. He picked a large leaf from an enormous dock plant that grew nearby and blew his nose with a noise that sounded like a ship's fog horn.

"KIMON," he said. "LETSGOFINDALOG."

The children got up excitedly. The place that the Bunjee had described in his story did sound exactly like the place where they had seen their father, and if the river ran straight past it . . .

"Hang on a minute though," Andy said, holding Karen's arm. "Supposing the cave place is up river against the current?"

"It can't be," Karen replied. "Remember what Bunjee said about his family not quite reaching their destination and deciding to settle in the forest instead? Well, if he never reached it and has been wandering around here ever since, that means we might be quite near."

Andy nodded. "You're right," he said. "Let's see if we can find something to float on."

* * * * * *

Some way back from the river bank amongst the litter of rocks that lay at the foot of the towering cliff grew a tree of a similar type to the one which Andy bumped into when he first stepped out of the time machine. It had the same enormous girth and its bark was soft and fibrous, but here the similarity ended for on this tree the branches didn't start until the very top. It looked like a giant's umbrella. The branches stretched way, way out over the river below and amongst its thick green leaves there hung round yellowy fruits which were spiky and contained glossy brown nuts. It could well have been an ancestor of the present day horse chestnut except that it would have been impossible to play conkers with these, for each one stood at least as tall as a man.

The ground was scattered with fallen chestnuts. Some lay amongst the rocks, still encased in their yellowy husks and others lay brown and shiny, the husks having split in half with the impact of the fall.

When the children and Bunjee came trudging along the river bank and saw the chestnuts they were at first afraid. The spiky yellow cases lay crouched in the long grass like menacing animals about to pounce and the very size of the tree from which they had fallen was enough to send a shiver of awe down the spine.

They stared speechless for a moment or two, then Andy let out a long low whistle.

"Wowee, look at the size of those conkers!" he said. "If only the kids at school could see those."

He took a pace or two towards them, then stopped. From somewhere way above their heads they heard a soft snapping noise followed by a long barely audible rushing of air. A giant chestnut smashed with sickening force into the ground a little way to Andy's left. He flattened himself into the grass as one half of the spiky shell flew above his head and landed in the undergrowth behind him. The big brown nut spun up into the air and bounced off to settle amongst the rocks and the other half of the spiky shell splashed into the river and floated off downstream.

Bunjee shot out his trunk, grabbed Andy by the ankle, and hauled him back to where he and Karen were standing.

"HEYWATCHOUT," he said. "WUNOFDEM-TINGS," he pointed with his trunk, "COODGIVY-OOANASTILUMPONAHED."

"Phew, that was close," said Andy. "Thanks, Bunjee." He dusted himself down and looked off in the direction that the shell was floating. "Well," he said. "I think we've solved our transport problem."

The other two looked at him slightly puzzled, then

Karen said "Of course! What a super idea. There's no need to find a log now."

Bunjee still looked puzzled. "WAITAMINIT," he said. "WHYFORDONTWENEEDALOG?"

"We'll use the conker shells," said Karen. "Don't you see? They make marvellous boats and they're almost big enough for all three of us."

Bunjee started to nod vigorously. "DARNIT," he said. "WHYDIDINTEYEFINKOFDAT?"

Andy looked up at the sky. It was getting quite dark. The sun sat on the horizon and the trees cast long zebra patterns across the ground. The air was steadily getting chillier and he knew that it would be foolhardy to start their trip on the water before morning. He yawned and stretched his arms. It had been a long hard day.

"I think we'd better camp here for tonight and start tomorrow morning," he said.

Karen was eager to get on but she could see the sense in what Andy said. Suddenly she felt very tired.

"All right," she said. "Where shall we sleep?"

Bunjee pointed with his trunk. One of the chestnut husks lay propped up at one end by a small rock. It was out of range of any other falling chestnuts and there would be just room for the children to crawl underneath.

"DATLOOKSANICESAFEPLACE," said Bunjee.

They inspected it and agreed that it was a fine place to sleep. Bunjee waited till they were safely tucked up inside and then plodded off in search of food and a good place to park himself for the night. Before he had walked five yards the children were fast asleep.

Chapter Ten

A tiny brown creature, half bird, half lizard, sat high on a branch somewhere in the great still forest. He ruffled his feathers, blinked the sleep from his eyes, listened, then stared astonished at the first glimmer of the morning's light which appeared way off to the east. He listened again to the intense quiet that surrounded him, then with pounding heart and incredible daring he pierced the vast black silence with a tiny high pitched whistle. Then he sat back nervously on the branch overwhelmed by his own impudence. Far away, tucked deep in a mossy hollow a weird armour plated creature with long ears and webbed feet was jolted awake by the noise. He frowned in annoyance at not being first, took a deep breath and gave an answering croak. From down near the roots of the same tree came a loud cawing. Then a deep grunting noise rumbled out from another part of the forest.

Suddenly it seemed that the whole world was awake, each animal large or small opening its throat in a deafening cacophony of sound to welcome the new day.

Down below in the clearing by the river the two children stumbled sleepy eyed from the shelter of the upturned chestnut husk. They listened for a while in amazement to the prehistoric dawn chorus, then turned to the river to wash away the remains of sleep.

They ate a hearty breakfast of berries, then together and with much effort they pulled two of the husks up to the river bank ready for launching. Andy cut two large stiff leaves from a plant to use as paddles, threw them into their new boats, and sat down on the grass beside his sister. They waited impatiently for Bunjee to turn up.

Karen felt as though all the butterflies in the world were holding a dance inside her stomach. She felt somehow very close to her father since Bunjee had told his story. It was possible that the sandy place with the caves was just around the next bend in the river. She prayed that her father had stayed in the same spot. It would be terrible if they found the place again but he had moved off somewhere else.

Andy stood up suddenly and pointed upwards through the trees. It was getting much lighter now. The sky was misty grey and, silhouetted against it, came Bunjee, trunk inflated and long red hair flowing in the wind, sailing down towards them. He landed with uncanny accuracy and a light thud right beside them, smiled broadly and said

"OKAYWOTWEWAYTINFOR."

"Oh thank goodness you're here," said Karen. "We want to be on our way."

Andy pointed at one of the chestnut husks. "Bunjee, I don't think we'll all fit into one boat after all, so if you sit in this one and hold on to the other one with your trunk we'll be able to stay close together."

"GOODTINKINGANDEE," said Bunjee and started pushing his boat into the water. The other two steadied it while he laboriously clambered in. It was fairly hard work getting both boats launched for the water was running extremely fast, but after some difficulty they managed to push off from the bank, Bunjee clinging to the children's boat with his trunk.

They were immediately sucked into the middle of the river. The chestnut boats dipped and swayed alarmingly, and within seconds they were soaked to the skin. Straight away it was apparent that the two paddles that Andy had cut from the plant would be useless, the current was too fast. Bunjee's face had gone a kind of green colour, whether because he was scared stiff or because he felt seasick even he wasn't sure. He just clung desperately to the other boat, his eyes screwed up tight and his red hair plastered wetly across his face. The two boats swirled round and round each other pitching and tossing, and bucketing with such ferocity that it was difficult to know which was upstream, which was downstream, and even whether they were still the right way up.

Suddenly the river was split into two separate streams by a boulder which bulged from the water like a sleeping hippopotamus. Bunjee tried his hardest to hang on but his boat was swept through on one side of the rock and the children on the other. He was carried off on a much faster current, his face a mask of misery. Andy scooped desperately at the water with his paddle in an effort to catch Bunjee up but it was useless. They had been swept into a series of pools each with a small waterfall at one end so that their journey was made up of agonisingly slow drifting sections punctuated by fast spurts. Bunjee on the other side was hurtling along at breakneck speed, spinning like a top, and yelling for all he was worth.

"HEELP.! AHWANNAGETOFF!"

Rapidly he got further and further away from the children and with a last despairing call of "AHMTOO YUNGTODIE!" he disappeared from view. Karen and Andy paddled furiously until their arms ached but it was of no use. It was impossible not to go the way the river wanted them to go. Eventually they gave up the struggle and just sat back dejectedly in their little coracle and let the river have its way.

They drifted for hours. The forest was endless and monotonous but they were glad of its leafy coolness, knowing that beyond the thick foliage above, the sun must by now be at its height. Two or three times they floated past large animals drinking at the river bank and once they even floated between the legs of a scaly monster that was so big it was like sailing under London bridge. They flattened themselves to the bottom of their shell, sure that they would be eaten. The monster saw them. Its great head bore down on them at the end of an impossibly long neck, sniffed at them curiously, then turned away and started eating grass from the opposite bank.

They had long since given up any attempt to try to direct their boat. The sun flickered through the gaps in the leafy canopy above. It had the same effect as of someone continually flashing a torch on and off in their eyes, so they lay back in the bottom of the shell with their eyes shut, drifting gently downstream, spinning occasionally as the little boat was caught up in a faster current, then slowing up again in the pools, bumping into rocks and dipping quickly down the small waterfalls. It became a monotonous rocking rhythm and Andy dozed off and dreamt about home and his mother and television sets and cooked meals and football and his own comfortable bed. Karen was thinking about Bunjee and wondering what had become of him. She hoped he was safe. Twice now he'd saved her life. It would be just awful if they never saw him again. Perhaps his boat had capsized and he had drowned. She wondered if he could inflate his trunk in the water and float. "Of course," she reassured herself. "If his boat did capsize he would float." Then she remembered the piranhas that Bunjee had spoken of. She shuddered and tried to put the thought out of her mind.

She put her arm up to her forehead. Her eyes hurt and she felt hot and uncomfortable. She wondered vaguely what had happened to the lovely cool breeze and then she became aware that the sun was no longer flashing on and off but was on all the time, shining blisteringly hot through her eyelids. She sat up quickly and looked around. They were out of the trees. The land on all sides was a yellow sandy colour. It was pitted with holes. In the ground and on the surrounding slopes large black caves yawned like the surface of a sponge.

"Andy!" she cried. "Andy! We're here! We're here!" She shook him roughly on the shoulder and he sat up blinking blearily. "We're back at the place where we saw Daddy!" she yelled in his ear, and pointed excitedly at the near bank. Andy stared around him, his mouth open with astonishment. He stood up making the boat wobble dangerously and shouted "YAHOOOOOOOO!"

Karen leapt to her feet and hugged him with glee. They did a little war dance, delirious with excitement, then sat down again as the boat lurched violently.

"It is the same place isn't it Andy?" Karen asked anxiously.

"I think so," he answered. "See, the river runs along parallel to the forest and look how straight the edge of the forest is. Don't you remember that?"

"Yes," said Karen. "The edge of the forest was in a straight line, but I don't remember seeing a river."

Andy frowned. He couldn't remember a river either. Maybe it veered off at right angles to the trees soon and the place where they had seen their father was further on.

Just then the boat bobbed over the lip of another small waterfall, twisted quickly between two large rocks and started for the first time in hours to accelerate. It was sucked once more towards the centre of the river. Once again they were quickly soaked through by the spray.

Andy cupped one hand to his mouth and yelled above the roar of the water. "If the river starts to go away from the line of trees we'll have to try to get off."

Karen shook her head to show that she couldn't hear. The noise of the water seemed much louder now than it had done before. In fact it was becoming deafening. It had the same reverberating, ear-drum shattering sound as a one-man band in a telephone box. The same roar as Niagara Falls. Karen stretched up as high as she dared and looked up ahead to see what was making all the din. Her heart almost stopped. About a hundred yards ahead the river did change direction, but not to the right or left as Andy had guessed it would, but down! All this huge expanse of rushing water simply disappeared down one of the great black holes in the ground.

It vanished in one eternal gurgling swallow into the inky black bowels of the earth like bathwater going down a gigantic plughole, and they were rushing towards it at breakneck speed!

She turned to warn her brother but saw by the horrified expression on his face that he had seen the danger too. She looked at the nearest bank. Too far to jump. She picked up one of the green leaf paddles from the floor of the boat and rammed the flat end into the water in an attempt to force their craft nearer the land. Andy grabbed the other paddle but it was of no use. The current was too strong. They had realised their danger too late. The little boat was sucked faster and faster towards the great dark hole. Suddenly it was on the very lip. The world dropped away from beneath them. Karen caught one last glimpse of her brother's white face and then she was tumbling over and over in the blackness, a sick knot of numbness in her stomach. She felt the numbness sweep up her body as she fell. A total lack of feeling in every limb. Everything, every jangling nerve, every sensation of fear, was forced up into her head and out in a long scream that was smothered completely by the deafening roar all around her. Suddenly she reached the other end of the waterfall. She had still been screaming and had not had time to take a breath. Her mouth filled with water as the gigantic liquid column rammed her deep down into the water below. She felt as though she was under a thick suffocating mattress and two dozen carthorses were doing a war dance on top of it. She was tossed and beaten and battered by a million different currents each trying to pull her a different way. Her lungs were bursting for air and she struggled feebly with her arms, trying desperately to swim out of trouble. She felt a terrific bang on the forehead as she hit the ground, then suddenly she was up at the surface and in the air and she could breathe. She put out her arms in the darkness and felt the cold slippery side of a rock protruding from the water and she clung to it spluttering and coughing and gasping and astonished that she was still alive. She wondered dimly whether Andy was too.

It was some time before she lifted her head and took stock of her surroundings. Her eyes had become more accustomed to the dark now and she could see that she was in a vast underground cavern. The waterfall was about forty yards away on her left. At the foot of it the water boiled and erupted, sending out a great wall of spray which she could feel against her face. High up in the roof of the cavern she could see what appeared at first to be the moon. A large yellow circle which let into the vast gloomy cavern a shaft of light that reflected on the wet walls and made another circle on the black water below. Then it dawned on her what it was. Another of the great holes in the ground that they had seen when they were on the river in the boat. "Thank heavens for this hole," she thought. "At least I can see."

About twenty yards in front of her was a rocky shelf that stood about a foot out of the water and stretched back to the far wall of the cavern. She decided to swim across to it. Her arms were getting tired hanging on to the rock and her legs numb from the cold water. She pushed off from the rock and started to swim. Just then something touched her on the back. She plunged to one side in terror, her heart once more up in her mouth. Something white floated a yard away. It bobbed and nudged gently against the rock that she had just left. She strained her eyes to see what it was. It turned slowly as the current pushed it against the rock and she saw the long golden hair floating in the water.

"Andy!" she cried. "Andy!" He was floating face downwards, his arms stretched out in front of him. Some air had lodged in the back of his shirt and this was ballooned out on his back above his belt.

Karen caught hold of one of his arms and turned him over. His face was a ghastly white, drained of all colour, except for his lips which had a blueish tinge. She cupped her right hand under his chin and swam backwards as quickly as she could to the rocky shelf she had seen earlier. It was the longest swim of her life. Her brother felt enormously heavy and there was quite an undertow caused by the waterfall which kept sweeping her away into the dark recesses of the cavern. Apart from this she was terribly tired and cold, her legs ached with fatigue and her brain felt numb. She had an overwhelming urge to float on the water and just drift off to sleep.

At last she reached the shelf. She clung on to the edge with one hand and summoning up her last ounce of strength, somehow she managed to push her brother up and onto the flat rocky surface above. He lay still and white on his back with his legs dangling in the water. Karen crawled out beside him, teeth chattering and trembling all over. She looked down hopelessly at her brother. What to do now? She tried desperately to think. Her brain seemed slow and sluggish. Perhaps she was too late anyway. She leaned forward and undid the top two buttons of his shirt, then loosened the belt of his trousers. It was coming back to her now. A lesson on life saving that she had when taking her swimming badge for the Girl Guides some time back.

She checked to see if she could detect any heartbeat or sign of breathing. It was very difficult with the waterfall making so much noise. Then she rolled him over onto his side, put her knee against his back and pressed her hands against his tummy, just below the rib cage. She relaxed then squeezed again. Quite a lot of water was coming out of his mouth. "My goodness," she thought. "He's swallowed half the river." She kept up the squeezing for a little while longer then let him roll onto his back again. "Better try the kiss of life now," she muttered to herself. She tilted his head back as far as it would go, to create as straight a line as possible between mouth and lungs, then pinching his nose between thumb and forefinger she took a deep breath and . . . "Don't you dare!" suddenly he was alive and propped up on his elbows and coughing and spluttering and gasping for breath and saying things between gasps like: "I don't want to be kissed! What d'you think you're playing at? Soppy woman! Ugh! Get off!"

Karen put her hands on her hips. "Well of all the ungrateful little beasts! I nearly drowned myself saving your life, I wish I hadn't bothered now!"

After another fit of coughing he said "Oh don't be silly. I'm grateful that you saved my life, of course I am, but honestly, there's a limit you know. You don't have to do all that soppy kissing bit. That's the trouble with girls, they always have to get all smoochy."

"Smoochy? You don't suppose I wanted to kiss you, do you? Huh! I'd rather kiss one of Bunjee's piranhas."

Andy looked dolefully out over the black water for a while then said "Bunjee, poor dear old Bunjee. I wonder what happened to him. Do you think he went down the hole like we did and got himself drowned?"

"I hope not," said Karen. She shivered. "I'm freezing! C'mon we'd better try to find a way out of

85

here before we both catch pneumonia."

Andy climbed to his feet and steadied himself against the wall. He still felt a little light headed after having been so close to drowning. His hand touched something cold and wet. Suddenly he felt a sharp burning pain shoot up his arm from his fingertips and he jerked his hand away from the wall with a shout.

"Ouch!" he yelled. "That hurt!"

Karen looked at him in amazement as he hopped up and down waving his sore hand in the air. He rushed across to the edge of the rocky shelf and plunged his hand into the water.

"What on earth are you doing?" she asked.

"Something on the wall bit me," he wailed.

"Bit you?"

"Well, stung me, whatever it did it hurt." He took his hand out of the water and inspected it. It was extremely red and two of the fingertips had large painful blisters on them.

"Wow!" breathed Karen, staring down at his hand. "Whatever did that?"

They walked back across to the wall and examined it closely. There was nothing there. Just the grey black rock, glistening wet with spray from the waterfall. Just then something moved low down where the floor and wall met. They stared down at it. It slid off the wall and round the angle onto the floor with a soft flopping noise. It was lighter here and the children managed to get a good look at it.

"It . . . it's like a big lump of jelly," said Andy.

"Maybe it's a jellyfish," said Karen.

"It's too big for a jellyfish – besides, when did you see a jellyfish that could climb up walls?" He pointed his finger. "By golly, it can certainly move fast whatever it is." The jelly crept across the rocky floor, making a rather nasty spluttering sound. It seemed to be moving around the children as though to avoid them.

"Hey," said Karen, pointing. "Look, there's another lump of the stuff." Andy looked where she was pointing. A much larger mass of the jelly like substance moved out of the shadows and slurped revoltingly towards them.

It was impossible to see how the jelly moved. It didn't have any visible means of propulsion. There were no legs or feelers. In fact it did not seem to have any organs at all. No stomach, no heart, no eyes. Just a transparent blubbery mass that somehow oozed and flowed across the ground or up the walls. The second piece of jelly stopped and the smaller patch moved quickly towards it. They touched, and suddenly there was only one large mass. They had merged together.

"Did you see that?" said Karen. "They just joined together like two puddles."

"It's incredible," mumbled her brother. "Look, it's moving again."

The larger mass flowed across the floor. Having joined together it seemed that the jelly had double the energy – the spluttering squelching sound became much louder and it moved along much quicker. The children stepped to one side to let it go past. Their footsteps echoed hollowly from the cavern walls. It turned and moved in their direction. They jumped back the other way and again it changed course.

"Watch out," said Andy. "It's after us!"

"Come on!" Karen grabbed his arm. "I don't like the look of that stuff. Let's get out of here."

They turned and walked along the shelf. The

glutinous mass wobbled after them. It was much darker here and the children had to walk along holding their hands out in front of them in case they should bump into the wall. Something touched Karen's ankle and she felt the same painful burning jolt that her brother had experienced a minute before.

"Uugh! There's more of the stuff just here!" she screamed. Holding hands they ran forward into the blackness. It didn't matter any more about bumping into walls, anything to get away from the horrible burning jelly.

They stumbled blindly about in the dark, panic rising in their throats, crashing into rocks, tripping over ridges in the floor. "Got to get away! Got to get away," Karen rasped. She reeled over sideways as something hard thudded against her shoulder and she fell painfully onto her knees. Andy stopped and pulled at her hand. "Come on, come on." he yelled.

"Shush! Be quiet and listen," Karen gasped.

They stood still in the black cavern and listened. At first all that they could hear was the sound of their own heavy, tortuous breathing and the now much quieter roar of the waterfall, and then they heard it and it seemed to be getting even louder than before and worst of all they weren't sure where it was coming from. The flubbering, flopping, squelching noise bounced and echoed from wall to wall around them until it seemed that they were surrounded. But one thing that they were sure of was that it was getting closer.

"This way!" Andy pulled at Karen's hand and they stumbled headlong over the edge of the shelf and into the fast flowing water below. They came up gasping and spluttering, holding desperately on to each other. Things were bad enough, but to be split up and have to face this kind of thing alone was too frightening to think of.

"Are you all right?" yelled Andy. His voice echoed off the walls and the question was asked at least another ten times.

"Apart from being cut and bruised all over and freezing to death, I think so," answered Karen.

"Just tread water and we'll let the current take us along. With a bit of luck, it might lead outside again."

"Fat chance of that," thought Karen, but didn't say so. She let the fast water carry her along and listened with growing terror to the sound of the waterfall getting further and further into the distance until it disappeared altogether and the noise of the jelly getting louder and louder all around her. The sickening noise bounced from wall to wall and she prayed silently that it was only an echo she could hear and not what it sounded like – masses and masses of the stuff clinging to every wall.

Andy broke into her thoughts. "Hey," he cried. "It's getting lighter." She turned and looked in the direction that the water was taking them.

Sure enough it was getting lighter. They were being carried along quite a narrow channel and ahead was another large cavern, but it was much, much lighter than the one that they had been in before, it seemed as though it was lit up by electricity, a great yellow glow at the end of the tunnel. They came out of the darkness and into the cavern and mercifully they could see. What a relief. Any kind of horror is much easier to bear if it can be seen. In the darkness its dreadful presence multiplies because it is unknown.

This new cavern was totally different to the last one. On either side was a rocky flat surface as before but from the floor there grew vast stalagmites which stretched up and up like gigantic pointed teeth and from the roof hung the stalactites, almost a reflection, pointing down and occasionally touching and forming huge pillars with the teeth below. As well as stalactites the roof of the cavern was liberally ventilated by holes, large beautiful holes that let in the sun. It shone through the holes, cutting the darkness like searchlight beams, criss-crossing, yellow lines against the black rock behind. It warmed the cold air, it caused a soft steam to rise from the water's edge, and it sparkled and glinted on the thick blubbery jelly that clung like an enormous foul carpet to practically every square foot of wall.

Andy felt his sister's grip tighten on his hand. She choked and waved a hand at the wall.

"Andy . . . the jelly . . . it's everywhere!"

Immediately a large section of blubber slid down the wall, across the floor past the base of a stalagmite and into the water. The rest of the jelly started making its revolting splut, splut, spluttering noise much louder than before and faster, a kind of excited chatter.

"That's it," thought Andy. "The jelly actually sounds excited."

Karen screamed. "It's in the water! It's coming for us!" Straight away another large section moved off the wall and oozed into the water and again the noise became louder.

Andy clamped his hand over his sister's mouth. "Be quiet," he hissed in her ear. She struggled against him, panic showing in her eyes. "Don't you see?" he tried to keep his voice as low as possible. "It only moves when one of us makes a sound. It must be attracted to noises."

"But it's in the water and I can't see it! . . . It disappears in the water!" She wrenched herself free and started swimming away from him against the current. He plunged after her and grabbed her by the hair.

"Let me go, let me go!" she screamed. Again he clamped his hand hard over her mouth. Over on the far wall another carpet of jelly slid towards the water. He looked frantically at the water around them trying to see if he could see any difference in texture, any sign that would tell him how close the jelly was. It just looked like water. But the first piece of the revolting stuff might be pretty close by now. Perhaps they were surrounded by it.

Again he whispered urgently into Karen's ear. "Please Karen, you must stop making a noise. The more you panic the worse it becomes. You must be quiet, it's our only chance!"

The urgency in his voice got through to her and gradually she stopped struggling. He took his hand away from her mouth and she nodded to him to show that she had calmed down a little.

Suddenly Andy felt a ferocious jolting pain on the side of his neck. The jelly had reached them. He lunged to one side, biting back the cry of pain that sprang to his lips.

"Listen Karen," he said desperately. "Do exactly as I say. We're both going to make as much noise as we can. When I shout 'now'!, duck down and swim underwater to the ledge with the stalagmites. Don't come up to the surface until you reach it, right?"

She looked bewildered but nodded. Andy started to shout as loudly as he could, and she opened her mouth and screamed.

The walls of the cavern seemed to dissolve. Great

masses of jelly suddenly came alive and with incredible speed slid down and across the floor, squelching and slurping into the water.

The children carried on screaming and shouting. Andy braced himself for the shock that would tell him that the jelly was almost upon them. It touched his ear and he gasped at the terrible hot pain that suddenly filled his whole head.

"NOW!" he shrieked and taking a deep breath he ducked under the water.

He could see quite clearly. The sunlight shafting through the holes in the roof overhead tinted the water a beautiful blue. Down below he could see the jagged floor of the cavern and he thought what a marvellous place it would be to swim if circumstances had been different. He glanced across at his sister swimming alongside. Her face screwed up, her cheeks puffed out and her long hair streamed behind her. They reached the wall and he held out the flat of his hand at Karen as a signal to wait. She clung to the wall, a small stream of bubbles escaping from her lips. Andy reached up with his hand, his teeth clenched together in anticipation of the pain that would come if the jelly were directly above. It was clear. His hand broke the surface and there was no jelly.

He tugged at Karen's arm and they both came up together, lungs bursting for air, and trying desperately not to make any noise.

Over in the centre of the lake, where they had just been, the water boiled and erupted. They could see the jelly now. It reared angrily into the air in great gouts then spattered back to join the one heaving mass on the surface. The noise was terrific but instead of being excited it seemed to have an angry quality about it.

The two children eased themselves out of the water, keeping their eyes on the jelly. Suddenly the spluttering noise died down and so too did the carpet of floating blubber. It lay still and quiet on the surface as though it was listening. Listening and waiting.

Andy pointed at one of the stalagmites. Water dripped from his clothes with every movement and it seemed to the children that the small droplets hit the floor with the noise of a tropical deluge. Still, it could not have been loud enough for the jelly to hear, there was no movement from the lake.

The stalagmite had joined high in the air to a stalactite and had formed a great pillar from floor to ceiling of the cave. About two feet from the top of the pillar was a hole, a beautiful hole that led out into the sunshine and freedom. If only they could reach it and get away from the loathsome jelly. Standing beside the pillar was a small stalagmite. Andy motioned Karen towards it. He cupped his hands between his knees for her to use as a step to hoist herself up with. She put her foot into his hands and he pushed her upwards as high as he could. She grasped the wet point of the stalagmite, found another foothold and, stretching out as far as she could, she leaned against the pillar. From here she could just reach the pointed end of a stalactite hanging down from the roof. She put out her foot, braced her back against the pillar and started edging herself upwards in a kind of sitting position.

Andy started to follow her. By leaping up he managed to get both hands around the top of the small stalagmite, then leaned out to brace himself against the pillar. Just then there was a loud snapping noise. The top twelve inches of the stalagmite broke off and Andy fell with a crash onto the rock below. His head cracked back against the foot of the pillar and he let out a bellow of pain.

Instantly the lake became alive. He stared horrified as the water suddenly heaved up and the surface became like boiling porridge. The jelly suddenly appeared over the edge of the rocky shelf. Transparent, shapeless, blubbery hands swarmed across that flat surface, pulling the rest of the huge mass behind. The spluttering noise started up again.

Up above, wedged between the stalactite and the pillar, Karen could contain herself no longer. "Come on!" she screamed. "Move or it'll get you!"

The shout pulled him out of his trance. He picked up the broken end of the stalagmite, put it on the ground nearer to the pillar, and used it as a step. The jelly was right up to him now. He looked down and saw that it was all over his shoe. He stepped onto the broken point and grabbed hold of the now flat top to the stalagmite. He pulled himself up so that he was sitting on the flat piece and once again leaned out so that he could hold on to the tall pillar. His foot felt hot. He looked down in amazement at what was left of his shoe. The leather had burned away almost completely. A smouldering bit of black toecap was all that remained. He kicked it off, his heart pounding. If the jelly could do that to a shoe what could it do to a human body? He shuddered violently. It was too awful to think about. You wouldn't last a second.

The jelly was creeping up the pillar now. It had changed its noise again and now sounded excited. Andy put out his foot and placed it on the tip of the stalactite, braced his back against the pillar and edged himself upwards as Karen had done. The stalactite looked terribly thin. "Don't break," he prayed.

"Please don't break."

He looked down. The base of the pillar was smothered in bubbling jelly and it was only a yard below him. He shuffled upwards as fast as he could. "Nearly at the top now. Keep going, keep going!" he muttered to himself. He felt sore all over. His neck, arm and hand had bad burns on them, he'd hurt his back and head when he fell, and he was scraping his hands to ribbons on the rough surface of the pillar. "Keep going, keep going," he said again.

"That's as far as we can go," Karen screamed at him. He looked up. She was wedged right up to the roof of the cavern. The hole was about two foot to one side of them and they could feel the warm sun against their faces. Karen stretched out a hand and could just reach the underside lip of the hole.

"There's nothing to hold on to," she said. She was trembling and tears were welling up in her eyes.

"Feel again!" Andy shouted from below. "There must be something to grip on to."

"There isn't!" came the reply. "We'll fall if we try swinging out that distance."

Andy looked down. The jelly was only six inches below him. The noise was dreadful now. The terrible excited spluttering like the chattering of old hags around a guillotine. He could feel the sweat trickling down the back of his neck. He looked up. Karen had gone!

"Karen!" he shrieked. "Karen! Oh, Karen!" She must have fallen, he thought. He edged himself further up the pillar. The jelly bubbled and hissed inches below him. He put his hand out to the lip of the hole. Karen had been right. There was no hand hold. He felt a sickening burning pain on the back of his leg. He jerked upwards away from it into the last two inches of available room, screwed his eyes up tight and waited for the end.

Something hard and rough gripped his wrist like a vice and pulled him off the pillar. His stomach lurched as he swung into space and then he was out in the sunlight. He opened his eyes and stared at the brown face close to his, the big soft eyes and the matted beard and hair.

"Hello Daddy," he said.

Chapter Eleven

"Well, well, well. What an incredible story." Mr. Winsborrow wiped a little more of his home-made ointment onto the burn on his son's neck, patted his daughter affectionately on the knee, and sat back on the ground near the fire. The two children snuggled up to their father and gazed into the flames happily.

Six hours had passed since their father had snatched them out of the cavern and away from the dreadful jelly. They had been so weak from fright and exhaustion that he had carried them across the sandy plain and up the hill to his cave. Here he had dressed their grazed elbows and knees, built up a large fire to warm them, and fed them from a store of fruit that he had at the back of the cave. He had insisted that they should not talk until they were fully rested and warm, but inevitably the questions tumbled out and anyway they were far too excited to rest. They had found their father. It had all been worth while after all. It seemed unbelievable that they could have escaped from all the horrors of the past few hours. Death had seemed so close at times, but now they had accomplished what they had set out to achieve. They had found him – now all that remained to do was to get home somehow.

Karen gave her father another squeeze. "But how did you find us?" she asked.

He smiled down on them. "It was just a fantastic bit of luck," he said. "Ever since I arrived at this place it has been my habit to walk across to the forest once a day to collect fruit. I was on my way back today when I heard you screaming and yelling down in the cavern. At first I thought it was some kind of prehistoric animal making the noise, but I looked down the hole and I couldn't believe my eyes when I saw you two down there."

"But why didn't you shout to let us know you were there?" said Andy.

"I did," replied Mr. Winsborrow. "But you were making such a racket you didn't hear me. When you ducked under the water I rushed back to the forest to cut a vine. I thought I'd lower it down to you to pull you out. When I got back of course you were both at the top of the pillar. I yelled and shouted but that jelly stuff was making such a din that you still couldn't hear me. Luckily you stuck your hand out and I was able to haul you up."

He hugged them both again for the hundredth time in the last hour and carried on. "You know, when you first appeared and the pterodactyl carried you off, I was so sure that you would be eaten. Oh, it was terrible. There was nothing I could do to help you. And now, here you are alive and well. You've been so very brave, enduring all that you have done, and so very clever getting here in the first place."

"But what about you Daddy?" said Karen. She leaned over and put another branch on the fire. "Have you been in any danger at all?"

Mr. Winsborrow scratched his head. "Well, I've had nothing like what you have had to go through. A tyrannosaurus had a peek into my cave one night, and

I have been chased by a couple of pterodactyls on my way to and from the forest. But nothing worth mentioning after your tales." He paused for a moment, then said, "Strangely enough, I was attacked several times today by a very sinister creature. Unfortunately I didn't have the fire going at the time. The wild creatures around here are terribly frightened of fire. But today I didn't light it. I was sitting down on a rock eating my lunch when this horrible creature attacked from the air. I managed to scramble out of its way and was able to drive it away by throwing stones at it. But it has tried again and again to get close to the cave. I only hope the fire will keep him at bay from now on."

Andy shuddered. "Can't we make a run for the forest now? Let's find the time machine now and go home. I'm sick of strange creatures attacking us. I want to see Mum."

Mr. Winsborrow smiled. "We all want to see your mum," he said. "But look outside, it's dark and there are all kinds of fierce animals prowling about at night. Be patient and wait till the morning."

"I suppose you're right," said Andy. Suddenly he felt terribly tired. He looked across at Karen. Her eyes were drooping too. "I think I'm going to go to sleep now," he said. He lay down beside the fire and closed his eyes. Karen needed no second bidding. She lay down beside her brother and cradled her head in her arms.

"Goodnight kids," said Mr. Winsborrow. He leaned over and kissed them both. "And thank you so much for having the courage to come and rescue me. I'm very proud of you both."

"Goodnight Dad," they said.

Mr. Winsborrow stood up and looked down on his

two sleepy children. He smiled happily and walked across to the pile of logs at the entrance to the cave. He started walking back and forward carrying logs and building up the fire for the night. Suddenly at the entrance to the cave he stiffened and stood staring out into the darkness. There was a faint clatter of rocks. Quietly Mr. Winsborrow walked back into the cave. He bent down beside the two sleeping children and shook them gently awake.

They looked up at him uncomprehendingly and Karen opened her mouth to speak. Mr. Winsborrow put his finger to his lips.

"SSSH!" he whispered. "Don't make any noise. The creature I told you about is outside again and he's coming straight towards the cave. Pick up a few rocks and we'll try to get rid of it."

Silently the children got to their feet. They armed themselves with stones, then flattened themselves against the walls of the cave.

The blackness outside was intense. The silence was total. Karen could feel her heart thudding in her chest. Both children were wide awake and alert now. The new danger prickled their skin and sharpened the senses.

Outside there was another clatter of stones. "The creature must be making it's way over the small band of shingle that lies at the bottom of the flat rock," Andy whispered into his father's ear.

Mr. Winsborrow nodded, his eyes fixed on the cave entrance. There was another long silence then quite clearly the three in the cave heard a kind of slurping noise as though the creature was licking something. Then . . . THWOK! THWOK! THWOK! THWOK!

Another silence, then a voice said

"ULLO! ISDERENNYBODYINDERE?"

"Bunjee!" yelled the children.

Mr. Winsborrow was almost bowled over as the children rushed past him and out of the cave entrance. He stood with a look of absolute astonishment on his face as they came back hugging and kissing a huge, hairy, elephant like creature.

"Daddy," they said in unison. "This is Bunjee."

Bunjee took a couple of steps backwards when he saw Mr. Winsborrow. He pointed at him accusingly with his trunk.

"HEFREWSTONESATMYED," he said.

"Oh, he didn't mean to," said Andy. "He thought you were an enemy, he's never seen a Bunjee before."

"EYE'DNEVERSEENIMBEFOUR," said Bunjee. "BUTEYEDIDN'TFROWSTONESATHISED."

"Daddy, if it hadn't been for Bunjee we'd both be dead by now," Karen said. "He saved our lives."

Mr. Winsborrow held out his hand and took a tentative step forward. "I'm sorry," he said. "I . . . I didn't know."

Karen turned to Bunjee. "Please, Bunjee, Daddy thought that you were a fierce animal coming to attack him. He knows better now. Please be friends."

Bunjee hesitated a moment longer. Then he smiled, shook Mr. Winsborrow's hand with his trunk and said "PLEESTAMEECHA."

They brought Bunjee into the cave. He didn't like the fire very much so he plugged himself comfortably onto the wall near the entrance.

Of course, sleep was forgotten again. The children and Mr. Winsborrow bombarded Bunjee with questions. What had happened to him after he'd been parted from them on the river? And had he fallen over the edge of the waterfall? Had he met the burning jelly?

Bunjee told them that he had managed to avoid being sucked into the caverns by inflating his trunk and floating over the hole. He had wandered about the sandy plain looking for eggs because he was terribly hungry, but he hadn't been able to find one pterodactyl's nest. Then he saw Mr. Winsborrow outside the cave. He had been terribly excited. He'd found Karen and Andy's father for them. But every time he'd tried to approach the cave Mr. Winsborrow had thrown stones at him.

Mr. Winsborrow shuffled his feet uncomfortably and looked embarrassed again.

"BUTEVERYFINGSOHKAYNOW," said Bunjee. He nodded at Mr. Winsborrow. "ANWEERALLFRENS."

"But Bunjee," said Andy. "Haven't you had anything to eat since we saw you on the boat?"

"NOPE."

"Nothing at all?" said Karen.

"NOPE."

Mr. Winsborrow rushed to the back of the cave and came back carrying an armful of fruit. "You poor old thing," he said. "Here, tuck into this."

Bunjee looked down in horror at the fruit.

"YUCK!" he spluttered.

"He doesn't eat fruit — only eggs," said Karen.

"EYEDON'TMEENTOBEROOD." Bunjee looked at Mr. Winsborrow apologetically.

"I've got it," said Mr. Winsborrow suddenly snapping his fingers. "I came across some eggs at the back of a cave the other day."

"Where?" asked the other three together.

"The cave's further along the hill," he said. "I'm afraid we'll never find it in the dark – can you hang on till the morning, Bunjee?"

Bunjee nodded and licked his lips. "ROLLONBREKFUSS," he said.

Once again they settled down to sleep, the three Winsborrows around the fire and Bunjee on the wall. The fire crackled and sparked and cast weird dancing shadows on the craggy walls, and as the fire dwindled the shadows too seemed to tire and dance less energetically until they lay still. The dull red glow of the fire died slowly, but before it was gone it was replaced by the soft growing light of the new morning.

* * * * * *

Bunjee watched the sunrise and heard the distant dawn chorus from the forest on the other side of the plain. He had been awake for hours. The gnawing hungry ache in his stomach kept him from sleeping. He waited patiently on the wall for the others to wake up. They lay huddled up beside the dead fire, Mr. Winsborrow snoring softly through his thick matted beard.

Bunjee thought wistfully about the eggs that Mr. Winsborrow had spoken of the previous night. Another pang of hunger echoed across his empty stomach.

"Won't they ever wake up?" he thought. He coughed politely. "AHEM!"

The three figures slept on. He sneezed, a little louder. "ATCHOOOO!"

There was no response.

104

"More volume," he thought to himself. "AAAACHOOOOOOOOOOOOOOOOOO!"

Andy rolled over onto his side and muttered something in his sleep. Mr. Winsborrow carried on snoring and all three slept on.

"This calls for desperate measures," thought Bunjee. "I'll give them the Bunjee in distress call that I was taught when I was little." He took a deep breath, opened his mouth as wide as he could (which was incredibly wide) and yelled "YAAAAAAAAAAAAAAAANNNOOOOOOOOOOOOOOOOPPRRROOIINNNGGYIPPEEEYIPPEEYIPPEEYIPPEEHOOOOOOOOOOWANGWANGWANGWANGWANGYYYOOWIPPROOOOIIIIOOONNK!"

Before he was half way through the others were up on their knees, wide awake with their hands clasped over their ears. Andy looked up anxiously at him.

"Whatever's the matter Bunjee? Are you all right? Are you in pain?"

"OOPSAH'MSORRY," said Bunjee. "DIDEYEWAKEYOOUP?" He looked at the three anxious faces innocently. "EYEMUSTAVESNEEZED," he said.

Mr. Winsborrow stretched his arms above his head and yawned. "That was some sneeze." He got up and wandered across to the cave entrance where he stood scratching his head and rubbing the sleep from his eyes. Then after what seemed an eternity to Bunjee he turned and said "Ah well, who's ready for some breakfast?"

"DATSOUNDSAGOODEYEDEEAH!" said Bunjee quickly as though he'd only just considered it.

"Oh Bunjee!" Mr. Winsborrow clapped his hand to his head. "I'm sorry, you must be starving. No wonder you were making all that noise. Well, hang on, I'll go and see if I can steal those eggs for you now." He picked up a large knobbly club from the back of the cave and strode purposefully out into the sunlight.

The children made themselves busy laying some fruit out on a large flat rock that served as a table. Ten minutes later Mr. Winsborrow staggered back into the cave carrying five enormous eggs. Three of them were orange spotted pterodactyl eggs, the other two were a bright turquoise blue with small flecks of white. These two had a thick layer of dust on them.

"Open up, here comes breadfast," said Mr.

Winsborrow. Bunjee smiled happily and opened his mouth. The three pterodactyl eggs disappeared in rapid succession.

"YUMMYYUMMY," said Bunjee, smacking his lips.

"Here comes pudding," said Mr. Winsborrow, picking up one of the turquoise eggs and wiping the dust from it.

Bunjee opened his mouth again then a startled look spread across his face, he gave a little cry, shut his mouth like a trap and fell off the wall onto his face.

The other three looked down at him in amazement.

"Whatever's the matter now?" asked Karen.

Bunjee staggered clumsily to his feet. Gently he took one of the blue eggs out of Mr. Winsborrow's hand. He held it up in front of his face, his eyes widening with every second. At last he spoke.

"DEMSNOTTERRYDAKTILSEGGS," he said.

"No?" said the others.

"NO," said Bunjee. "DEMSBUNJEEEGGS!"

"Bunjee eggs?" echoed the others.

"DATSWOTEYESED – BUNJEEGGS!"

"I found them way at the back of the cave," said Mr. Winsborrow. "They weren't with the pterodactyl's eggs."

"That's fantastic!" said Andy. "One of your family must've got as far as this place after all, when they all came down the river."

Bunjee nodded enthusiastically.

"How super," said Karen. "What are you going to do with them, Bunjee?"

Bunjee put the two eggs into his mouth. His cheeks bulged out like two balloons but he still managed to smile happily.

"You're surely not going to eat them?" asked Andy.

The reply was a bit muffled but they understood him to say that Bunjees always hatched their eggs out in their cheeks.

"But they're ancient. Surely they won't hatch now."

Bunjee didn't reply, he just nodded at them all with a knowing smile between the bulging cheeks as though to say "You wait and see."

So the children and Mr. Winsborrow ate their breakfasts and when they had finished Mr. Winsborrow said "Well kids. Do you think that you could find the place where your machine is hidden again?"

"I've been thinking about that," Andy said. He pointed across the plain at the forest beyond. "You can't see it from here, but somewhere over there there is a break in the forest. A long path that was made by a monstrous animal that forced its way through the trees when we first arrived here. If we run across to the forest and walk along the edge I'm sure I'll recognise it when I see it."

"Fair enough," said his father. He picked up his club and took a last look around his cave. "Well," he said, "shall we go?"

They all felt tremendously excited. Perhaps soon they would be back in their own time and their own home. They longed to see Mrs. Winsborrow again. She must have given up all hope of ever seeing her children and her husband again. Oh, what a surprise it was going to be.

Bunjee insisted on coming with them to the forest to see them off and although it slowed up the perilous journey across to the trees they were glad of his cheerful company and felt protected by his enormous bulk.

In fact the journey across was incident free. They saw two pterodactyls, but they were far away in the distance, wheeling around the sky like giant vultures.

Once in the shade of the giant trees, they rested for a while then slowly walked along the dead-straight line of trunks hoping to find the opening that would lead them back to their time machine. The children kept looking towards the caves on the far side hoping that they would recognise their position. Perhaps they were walking in the wrong direction. Maybe the path was the other way. Two or three times they came to gigantic openings in the line of trees that must have been made by the same creature, but these swerved either to the right or the left and they felt sure that the path that they had travelled along was dead straight. It was just when they were sure that they were going the wrong way that they came to it. There was no mistaking it. A great roadway torn through the forest, dead straight as far as the eye could see. Gigantic holes in the ground that had once held the roots of the enormous trees. Huge trunks that lay sprawled in all directions. The only difference that the children could see was that the leaves on the branches were now shrivelled and hung limply downwards.

Eagerly they started scrambling over the fallen trees, down into the hollows, pushing through the thick dead foliage. They found that they got along a lot quicker when Bunjee inflated his trunk to its fullest extent. In this way, when they arrived at a particularly large tree that had to be climbed over all they had to do was get together and pat Bunjee up and over as though they were playing with a gigantic balloon. But he was extremely slow when they had to scramble through any thick branches. Getting his huge bulk between some of the narrow gaps was very hard work and he was terribly anxious not to break the precious eggs that were in his mouth.

When they had been travelling along in this way for about three hours they stopped to have a rest. Karen slumped down onto the ground and rested her back against a branch. The other three leaned against a fallen tree. Mr. Winsborrow wiped his brow with his forearm.

"Do you think we are anywhere near the place?" he asked.

"We must be fairly close," said Andy. "Oh drat! I wish I'd marked the spot before we left."

"Don't worry," said his father. "I'm sure we'll find it soon. I'm afraid I can't help much. Remember, I arrived in the same spot as you did when I first came here. But I didn't have my time machine with me and I didn't have this long path in the trees to guide me. Things look very different now."

Karen got to her feet. "I'm hungry," she said. "I wonder if there are any fruit trees nearby." She wandered off further down the path.

Andy looked across at Bunjee. "You're very quiet Bunjee," he said. "Is there anything the matter?"

Indeed, Bunjee had been looking more and more downcast the further they had travelled along the path.

"AHMGOINTUMISSYOOLOT," said Bunjee. "THATSALL."

"Oh don't be sad," said Andy. "We'll come and see you from time to time."

Bunjee put on a brave smile. He knew that the Winsborrow family had had a pretty rough time and that they were really only being kind. He felt sure that they would rather do anything than return to this savage place. His thoughts were interrupted suddenly by a sharp cry from further along the path. He looked round. Karen was standing on a large grey rock waving her hands and shouting excitedly.

"She's found it!" yelled Andy. All three started to run, tiredness forgotten. The obstacles in their path were cleared easily as they rushed excitedly to the foot of the grey rock.

Sure enough, there it was, just as they had left it. The clutter of wires and tubes and bits of household paraphenalia, the pieces of carport support, the breadbin lid, all welded together and looking like some mad scientist's nightmare. Andy opened the door. "Don't let's wait any longer," he said. "Let's get home."

There was a loud sniff. He looked round. Bunjee stood by the grey rock, a large tear rolling down his trunk. They all walked slowly across to him.

"Goodbye Bunjee," Andy said. He squeezed the big creature affectionately. "And thanks for everything."

"Bye bye Bunjee darling," said Karen, wiping a tear from her own eye.

Mr. Winsborrow walked forward, his hand outstretched. He opened his mouth to speak. Suddenly the smile vanished from his face and was replaced by a look of horror. He wasn't looking at Bunjee now but over his shoulder. They all whirled round. The grey rock that Karen only moments before had been standing on was moving. It rose up about six feet in the air and for the first time they saw that it had a row of sharp pointed claws and scaly sides. It wasn't a rock at all, it was a gigantic foot. Towering above them like an enormous building was a tyrannosaurus.

The foot crashed down again making the earth tremble. The monster leaned forward, opened its throat and gave a tremendous ear shattering roar. For a long moment the four stood petrified with fear. Then Mr. Winsborrow grabbed the two children and bundled them towards the time machine. "Come on!" he yelled. "Get in!"

They raced forward. Karen scrambled through the door first, followed by Andy. Mr. Winsborrow had to squeeze into an impossibly small space. He was crouched over the seat, his face pressed against the wall and his knees wedged against Andy's back. Somehow they managed to close the door.

Outside the monster was ripping trees from the ground in an effort to get at them. Great gouts of earth cascaded from the roots and crashed down on the flimsy machine. It was deafening inside. Andy couldn't get his hands to work quickly enough.

"Hurry, Andy! Hurry!" screamed Karen. Her voice was smothered almost completely by the roar of the monster as it stretched out a huge clawed hand to pick up the machine.

The studded seat belt was in position and they had the little plugs in their ears. The indicator was set for the right time. Andy pushed the final switch. The machine rocked crazily as something outside hit it hard. The motor noise rose to a shrieking crescendo.

Then they heard two more noises on the outside metal skin of the machine. THWOK! THWOK!

Chapter Twelve

Police Constable 358 Arthur P. Sprocket, shivered. The rain drizzled relentlessly down and he could feel it dripping from the back of his helmet onto the collar of his cape and down the back of his neck. He sighed and wished he was back at the station warming himself by the electric fire and sipping hot tea instead of being stuck here guarding an empty garage. "Still, that's what the Inspector wants," he thought to himself.

Two or three more sightseers had arrived and were goggling open mouthed at the house. One of them even had a camera and was taking photographs of it.

"Come along now, move along," said Constable Sprocket, walking down the short drive to the gate. "there's nothing to see here."

"Have they found those two poor little children yet?" said one of the people, an old lady with a large flowered hat.

"Move along now," said Constable Sprocket again.

"Who'd 'ave thought that that nice Mrs. Winsborrow could've got rid of her husband and her two children like that?" said the woman.

"I always said there was something sinister about her," said a man in a brown coat standing next to her. "She had shifty eyes."

Constable Sprocket frowned. "Now then, now then, we have no proof that Mrs. Winsborrow has er ... disposed of her husband and children," he said, then added the ominous word "Yet." He waved his arm. "So come along, no more gossip. Move away please."

The small group of people moved on down the street muttering to themselves and pointing back at the house. Constable Sprocket walked back through the drizzle and took up his position outside the garage door again.

"A strange case," he thought to himself. "First of all, the husband disappears mysteriously four months ago, and his wife makes up some cock and bull story of a time machine exploding, and then the children disappear too and the woman tries to make out that the same thing had happened to them. She must think we policemen are stupid."

Inspector Bland came out of the house with two fingerprint experts and Constable Sprocket sprang smartly to attention. "Any luck, Sir?" he asked.

"Well, we've searched the house completely, 358," said the Inspector. "But I'm afraid that we haven't come across any really good clues. We've searched the garden thoroughly too; nothing there."

"What about the garage Sir?"

"Yes, we've had a look in there of course. Empty apart from a lot of old bits of junk. We found some drawings of a strange type of machine, but she could have put them there to try to make us believe her story."

"A very crafty woman," said Constable Sprocket.

"Very," agreed the Inspector. "Well, 358, you stay here and keep the noseyparker sightseers away. I'm going back to the police station to see if I can get a confession out of Mrs. Winsborrow."

"Right Sir, very good Sir. Leave it to me Sir." said Constable Sprocket.

Just then there was a knocking noise from the inside of the garage door.

"Pardon, 358?" said the Inspector.

"It wasn't me Sir," said Constable Sprocket.

The knocking noise came again from inside the garage.

"I think it's coming from in there Sir," said one of the fingerprint men.

"It can't be. We've just searched in there and it was empty." Inspector Bland pushed past the Constable, grabbed the door handles and pulled open the doors.

"Good gracious," said Andy. "The Police! What are you doing here?"

The four policemen stared, unable to speak, at the three Winsborrows. Inspector Bland's mouth had dropped open and a small gurgling noise came out of it.

"Yes, what ARE you doing here?" asked Mr. Winsborrow politely.

There was still no sound from the policemen. Inspector Bland tried to speak but all he could manage was more gurgling.

There was a shuffling sound from the darkness of the garage. A huge, red, hairy creature with a trunk and enormous bulging cheeks suddenly appeared in the doorway.

"ULLO," it said. "DISLOOKSANICEPLACE."

This was altogether too much for the police.

"AAAAAAGH!" said Inspector Bland.

"MUVVER!" said Constable Sprocket.

The two fingerprint men turned and ran. The

Inspector and the Constable staggered backwards, goggle eyed over the unkempt front lawn and fell with a great splash into the fishpond.

"WOTSAMATTERWIFFDEM?" said Bunjee.

* * * * * * *

Mrs. Winsborrow sighed wistfully and went back to her knitting. The policewoman would be bringing her lunch soon. But she didn't feel much like eating. Not that the food wasn't nice. It tasted fine, and the policewoman had been very kind to her. But it was terrible being in a prison cell and really awful to be in there because they suspected her of having got rid of her husband and children.

She looked around her bare little cell gloomily. How could they think such a thing? Her family were the most important thing in her life, she wouldn't harm them. Still, it must've seemed a pretty odd kind of story to the police. "They must think I've gone off my rocker, going on about time machines," she thought to herself.

Her needles clicked on. The garment she was working on had started out to be a cardigan for the nice kind policewoman who brought her meals, but somehow because she was distracted by worry, it had gone on and on, growing longer and longer with every day that she was kept in custody. It trailed over the cell floor, yard after yard of cardigan until it covered practically every inch of floor space, and would have been better used as a carpet.

There was the sound of a key in the cell door lock. "Ah, that'll be lunch," thought Mrs. Winsborrow.

The door opened. Inspector Bland (the man who

had arrested her) stood in the doorway. He was soaking wet. His hair was plastered down on his forehead. Green pond weed hung like a necklace around his neck and a lily leaf was perched on top of his trilby hat. He squelched into the cell. Mrs. Winsborrow got the distinct impression that he wasn't very well.

"Mrs. Winsborrow," he said. "I've got some rather good news for you."

Chapter Thirteen

"No, I'm sorry, he says definitely no," said Mr. Winsborrow into the telephone. "Bunjee has done enough television interviews ... What? ... Yes, I know the public want to see more of him. ... But he was on your show only last week talking about pre-historic times, and he was on the radio last night ... Yes ... Yes ... No, I'm sorry."

He hung up and walked back into the kitchen where Mrs. Winsborrow and the two children sat eating breakfast. The kitchen window was open so that Bunjee could join in on the conversation. He was plugged onto the wall at the side of the house.

"Who was it this time?" asked Mrs. Winsborrow.

"It was the B.B.C. again. They want Bunjee to appear on the Bernie Cookson Show. I told them no."

Bunjee's face peeped round the edge of the window. "DIDYOOTELLUMABOWTDEEGGS?" he asked.

"Yes," nodded Mr. Winsborrow. "I told them. I'm afraid Bunjee old chap that like it or not you have become a celebrity."

"I think you did the right thing saying no," said Karen. "Bunjee is going through a crucial time at the moment hatching his eggs. It would be terrible if anything happened to them just because of a rotten old television interview."

There was a knock on the front door. Mr. Winsborrow got up from his breakfast for the umpteenth time and opened the door. It was, as he expected it would be, the Press again. A group of six reporters and three cameramen stood on the doorstep.

"Good morning, Mr. Winsborrow, I am Mory Flayplate of the Evening Globe. Would it be possible to speak to Mr. Bunjee?"

"No," said Mr. Winsborrow.

"Aw please, only for a minute!"

"You spoke to him yesterday."

"Yes, but . . ."

Mr. Winsborrow shut the door and went back to his breakfast.

It had been like this ever since they got back to the present day two months ago. First of all the papers had been shrieking the headlines: FAMILY BRING STRANGE MONSTER HOME FROM THE PAST! Then it was: ARMY ON ALERT IN CASE OF MONSTER ATTACK. Soon after it was: PRIME MINISTER TO MEET FRIENDLY MONSTER.

The house had been beseiged by people eager to catch a glimpse of Bunjee. T.V. cameras churned up the front lawn. Radio interviews were given in the kitchen. Scientists called and prodded Bunjee with strange instruments and asked thousands of questions about the past. Hundreds of pounds were offered by newspapers for exclusive firsthand accounts of the great adventure plus photographs of the family, the machine and Bunjee. These were turned down. A man who owned a circus had the cheek to ask if Bunjee would join his travelling troupe.

Bunjee had not liked any of this. He had taken it all

with his usual good humour and manners, but he hated being stared at. After much pleading by the T.V. companies he had been on television a few times, suffered the hot lights and the humiliation of a studio audience laughing at his appearance. He had good humouredly answered stupid glib questions, and came home at night to crowds of sightseers, pressmen, autograph hunters and people who wanted a lock of his hair, waiting around the house, not giving him a moment's peace

The family had tried to protect Bunjee as much as was possible. They had pleaded with everybody to leave him alone, but wherever they went they were followed.

Mr. Winsborrow had been to America and Russia to give lectures on time travel. The leading scientists of these two countries had pored over the machine, making notes, taking photographs. Money had been offered for the secret of how to travel through time and had been turned down. The Winsborrow family were never off the front pages.

All this had been very exciting at first. Signing autographs and having their photographs taken had made them feel like film stars. But after a time the family began to get weary of it. The never ending questions and the crowds of goggling sightseers always gathered around the front gate of their house wore them down and it seemed that there was no escape from it.

Feeding Bunjee had been a problem at first. There were of course no pterodactyl eggs to give him so he had to eat ordinary chickens' eggs. His normal consumption was three crates a day. At night time he slept on the back wall of the house. He was far too big to be brought into the house and anyway he said he preferred it out there.

The two Bunjee eggs he assured everybody were doing fine, and when he was out giving interviews on the television or radio, Mrs. Winsborrow kept them warm in the oven.

Mr. Winsborrow sat down again at the breakfast table. He looked down at his now cold bacon and egg, then up to the window at Bunjee.

"It was the newspaper people again," he said.

"I wish that they would leave us alone," said Andy. "After all, it's been two months now. We've told them all they could possibly want to know."

"Well, they can jolly well lump it while Bunjee is hatching his eggs," Karen said crossly. "He needs all the peace and quiet he can get."

Mrs. Winsborrow poured out another cup of tea for herself and said in a low voice so that Bunjee would not hear,"I just hope he's not kidding himself. I can't see how those eggs could have stayed all that time at the back of the cave you found them in and not go rotten."

Her husband frowned down at the new pipe he was busy breaking in (his old one having been left in the pterodactyl's nest).

"You must remember," he said, lighting up and puffing out clouds of white smoke, "that Bunjees are rather strange animals. Perhaps their eggs stay dormant until someone comes along and warms them up."

"I hope so," said Andy.

They all looked across at the window. Bunjee smiled back at them from between the bulging cheeks and winked.

* * * * * *

Two days later one of the eggs hatched. Karen was woken very early in the morning by a frantic banging on the window. She leapt out of bed and pulled back the curtains. Bunjee was banging on the window with his trunk. His face was bright red with excitement and his eyes had a desperate 'come and help' expression.

"Is it . . . is it the eggs?" Karen asked anxiously. Bunjee nodded vigorously. Karen ran into her parents' room. "Wake up, wake up," she shouted. "The eggs are hatching!"

The blankets heaved up into the air. Mr. and Mrs. Winsborrow struggled into their dressing gowns. Andy raced in from his bedroom. "Are you sure?" he asked.

"Well, Bunjee seems sure enough," said Karen. "Come on, hurry! Let's get downstairs."

They tumbled headlong down the stairs and out of the back door. Bunjee had walked off the wall and was standing on the lawn. The two turquoise eggs were lying on the wet dewy grass and Bunjee was blowing on them with his trunk. Karen and Andy and their mother and father crowded round and stared down at the eggs.

"Is there anything we can do to help?" asked Mr. Winsborrow.

Bunjee shook his head and stopped blowing. He seemed to be listening. The others listened too. From inside one of the eggs there came a distinct KNOCK, KNOCK, KNOCKING noise. Bunjee bunched the end of his trunk up into a fist and knocked back on the shell.

There was another answering knock from inside. Bunjee smiled round at the others.

"DIDYOOHEERDAT?" he said happily.

He swung his trunk down on the egg and gave it a sharp smack. It fell into two halves like a chocolate Easter egg.

Sitting inside was a miniature Bunjee. A tiny pink, wrinkled creature that kept blinking its eyes at the light. It didn't have Bunjee's red hair. It didn't have any hair at all. It sat pink and naked and slightly wet with loose folds of skin that fell bloodhound style over its forehead. It put out a tiny tongue and started to lick itself all over.

"Aaaaaw!" said the Winsborrows all together.

"HULLOLITTILFELLA," said Bunjee.

At the sound of Bunjee's voice the little pink creature stopped licking itself, opened its eyes wide and stared round at the assembled company. When it saw Bunjee its little face cracked into a big smile.

"EEP – EEP – EEP," it said in a squeaky voice. "EEP–EEP."

"Here we go again," laughed Andy.

"AGEN AGEN," the tiny little creature said. It was immediately attentive. The little head cocked to one side. The tiny forehead creased up with concentration.

Karen smiled up at her mother who was standing just behind Bunjee. "Isn't that fantastic, Mummy?"

"MUMEEE." The newly hatched baby swung its head round and looked up at Bunjee. "MUMEE," it said again. "AW ... ELLOMUMEEE."

"MUMMY?" said Bunjee. He looked so astonished that the others started to laugh. Mr. Winsborrow leaned against the house wall and dabbed at his eyes with a handkerchief.

"What about the other egg, Mummy?" he said.

Bunjee looked from the newly hatched infant to Mr. Winsborrow. "DATSNOTFUNNY," he said. "AHMNOTAMUMMY."

He plodded across to the other egg and listened for a while. Then he picked it up and popped it into his mouth again. "NOPE NOPE," he said. "DISWUNSNOTDUNYET." He walked across to his crate of eggs that stood near the back door, picked out a large brown one and plodded back to the baby.

"OPENUPLITTILFELLA," he said. The baby opened its mouth wide and Bunjee dropped the whole egg into it. It smacked its lips. "COR!" it said.

* * * * * *

The other egg hatched that afternoon and they went through the same procedure. Both babies insisted on calling Bunjee MUMMY, much to his embarrassment, and both seemed to have insatiable appetites. In the two weeks that followed Mr. Winsborrow had to double the egg order at the local farm. The babies just ate and ate and ate. Bunjee explained that it was important for them to eat as much as they did in order to

124

grow as quickly as possible. A Bunjee was open to all kinds of dangers back in prehistoric times and had to be big to protect itself.

And grow they did. Within a fortnight they were three times as big as they had been when they were hatched. In time Mr. Winsborrow was buying the entire output of eggs at the farm and he was finding it extremely expensive.

When the newspapers got to hear about the two new Bunjees they renewed their efforts to get more photographs and more stories. The television cameras reappeared on the front lawn and life again became almost intolerable. Even at school there was no privacy. The newsmen would be waiting at the gate for the children and even took photographs of them through the window during lessons.

Meanwhile Bunjee was becoming increasingly unhappy. He wanted badly to be teaching the two youngsters how to walk up cliffs, how to hunt for eggs, and how to fly. This was impossible on the small housing estate where the Winsborrows lived and would have been impossible anyway because wherever they went they would be followed by the crowds.

One day Mr. Winsborrow called a family conference. They all grouped together around the kitchen table. Bunjee was in his usual position on the wall outside the window, and the two little Bunjees sat snug and warm on his stomach covered up warmly by his red hair.

They all waited patiently for Mr. Winsborrow to fill and light his pipe. This done, he looked round at his family, coughed, then began.

"I think you must all know why I've got you all in here to talk," he said.

The others nodded.

"Life is completely intolerable at the moment. We can't blame the T.V. people or the newsmen. After all, they are just doing their jobs. We have had a remarkable adventure and we have brought forward to this time an animal that nobody in the world knew even existed."

Bunjee smiled proudly as Mr. Winsborrow continued. "So naturally the world wants to know as much as possible about it. But even though the news people are only doing their jobs I think we all are getting just a bit fed up of not having any privacy."

They all nodded again.

"Personally, I would just like to live an ordinary life again. And although Bunjee has been very patient and goodnatured and has never complained, I have a feeling that secretly he longs to go back to his own time and do all the things that are natural for a Bunjee to do." He looked across at Bunjee. "Now be honest, Bunjee. That's true isn't it?"

Bunjee went slightly pink and nodded. "ONLEEFORDESAKEOFDECHILDRUN."

"We understand Bunjee," said Karen. "I think you'll be happier teaching the little Bunjees how to find pterodactyl eggs."

"Of course we understand." Andy stood up, leaned out of the window and patted Bunjee. "And if we teach you how to use the machine you can always come back to see us from time to time."

Bunjee's face lit up. "DATSTREW," he said. "EYENEVERTHAWTOFDAT."

"Well that's settled then," said Mr. Winsborrow. "We'll do it tomorrow."

126

Chapter Fourteen

"Ooh look," said the lady in the flowered hat. "Here they come now." She waved her umbrella at the house and there was a murmur of excitement from the other sightseers grouped around the front gate. "Yes, and they've got that big hairy thing with them," said the man in the brown coat.

"Oh, Mr. Bunjee," called another man with a camera around his neck. "Would you mind posing for a few photographs for the Morning Blurb?"

Mr. Winsborrow opened the garage doors and waited while Bunjee waved cheerfully to the crowd. There was the click and flash of a dozen cameras then Bunjee plodded into the garage, followed by Andy, Karen and Mrs. Winsborrow. The two babies clung by their trunks to Bunjee's red hair.

"Will you allow an interview later, Mr. Bunjee?" shouted a man with a tape recorder hanging from his shoulder.

"Maybe later," shouted Mr. Winsborrow, and closed the garage doors.

The next hour was spent showing Bunjee how to make the time machine work. He was a very intelligent animal and was soon able to recite the exact procedure.

"Well you're too big to go inside Bunjee, but you arrived here stuck to the outside of the machine so that's how you'll have to go back. The baby Bunjees can travel inside," said Mr. Winsborrow.

He smiled and shook Bunjee warmly by the trunk. "Goodbye, don't forget to come back and visit us someday."

Mrs. Winsborrow stepped forward. "Here Bunjee," she said. "I've knitted this for you." She held out a long knitted tube of wool. Bunjee nodded at it.

"JUSTWOTIVEALWAYSWANTID," he said, not having a clue what it was but too polite to say so.

"It's a trunk warmer for cold pre-historic nights," said Mrs. Winsborrow.

"EYENOTHAT," said Bunjee, much relieved. "TAVERYMUCH."

"Goodbye and thanks for everything." Karen and Andy squeezed Bunjee and kissed the end of his trunk. "See you soon," said Andy.

The two baby Bunjees were strapped securely into the machine. They squeaked their goodbyes and Mr. Winsborrow set all the dials to their proper setting.

Bunjee clambered up on the workbench then across onto the side of the time machine. He smiled down on the family below.

"TANKYOOFORAVINME," he said and Mr. Winsborrow pressed the final button.

It was a strange sight. The machine hummed into life and then slowly it and Bunjee just faded away. Karen was reminded of the Cheshire cat in *Alice in Wonderland*. The last thing to fade was Bunjee's smile.

128